Asperger Syndrome

ASPERGER SYNDROME

A GUIDE FOR EDUCATORS AND PARENTS

Brenda Smith Myles
and
Richard L. Simpson

pro·ed
An International Publisher

8700 Shoal Creek Boulevard
Austin, Texas 78757-6897

© 1998 by PRO-ED, Inc.
8700 Shoal Creek Boulevard
Austin, Texas 78757-6897

Library of Congress Cataloging-in-Publication Data

Myles, Brenda.
    Asperger syndrome : a guide for educators and parents / Brenda Myles, Richard Simpson.
       p.   cm.
    Includes bibliographical references and index.
    ISBN 0-89079-727-7 (alk. paper)
    1. Asperger's syndrome.   I. Simpson, Richard, L., 1945–
II. Title.
RC553.A88M97   1998   97–17269
616.89'82—dc21   CIP

This book is designed in Goudy.

Production Manager: Alan Grimes
Production Coordinator: Karen Swain
Managing Editor: Chris Olson
Art Director: Thomas Barkley
Designer: Lee Anne Landry
Copyeditor: Suzi Hunn
Reprints Buyer: Alicia Woods
Preproduction Coordinator: Chris Anne Worsham
Editor: Jennifer Knoblock
Production Assistant: Claudette Landry
Production Assistant: Dolly Fisk Jackson

Printed in the United States of America

2   3   4   5   6   7   8   9   10   01   00   99   98

CONTENTS

Preface vii

1   Understanding the Meaning and Nature of Asperger Syndrome 1

2   Assessing Students with Asperger Syndrome 13
    AUTHORED WITH JUDITH K. CARLSON

3   Teaching Academic Content to Students with Asperger Syndrome . . 43

4   Planning for Social and Behavioral Success 69

5   Planning for Life After School 97

6   Understanding Asperger Syndrome and Its Impact on the Family . . 115

References 133

Index 139

PREFACE

It was more than five decades ago that the Viennese psychiatrist Hans Asperger published a seminal paper wherein he described a group of children with a unique social disability (Asperger, 1944). The disorder he described continues to be known by his name—Asperger Syndrome. For decades the term was primarily used in certain sections of Europe, with virtually no mention in the United States. Times have changed. Currently Asperger Syndrome is used worldwide to describe individuals with significant social and language peculiarities who simultaneously reveal normal development and functioning in some areas of their lives. Indeed, there has been a dramatic increase over the past several years in the number of children and youth identified as having Asperger Syndrome.

In spite of the exponential increase in the diagnostic use of the term Asperger Syndrome in the United States and Canada, and the predictable interest among parents, family members, and professionals, there is an enormous lack of understanding regarding the disorder. This lack of understanding is directly related to a lack of information about the disability, including its relationship to other "autistic-like" conditions. It is clear that parents and professionals alike are struggling to learn more about Asperger Syndrome, especially about effective methods for assisting children and youth diagnosed with the disability. The Autism Resource Center at the University of Kansas Medical Center, with which we are associated, daily receives calls from parents, educators, and mental health providers who are seeking information and support for individuals diagnosed with Asperger Syndrome. Unfortunately, there are few resources available to satisfy the growing demand for information about Asperger Syndrome.

This need for basic information about Asperger Syndrome is the foundation of this book. We wanted to write a book that would be easily understood by both professionals and lay people; that would address basic issues related to the characteristics of children and youth with the disorder; and that would outline basic methods to facilitate the growth and development of children and youth with Asperger Syndrome in the home, school, and community.

This book consists of six chapters. Chapter 1 provides an overview of Asperger Syndrome, including definitions and characteristics. Chapter 2 focuses on educational assessment and planning for students with Asperger Syndrome. Chapter 3 addresses basic academic support measures, and Chapter 4 focuses on social enhancement and behavior management methods appropriate for children and youth with Asperger Syndrome. Chapter 5 offers information and suggestions for helping youth with Asperger Syndrome make the transition from home and school settings to adult life. Finally, Chapter 6 explores the impact on families of individuals with Asperger Syndrome. This final chapter is authored by several parents, who chose not to identify themselves by name. Each of the chapters is written in a straightforward style. The book contains minimal review of research; references are included only where required. Although there are potential problems with this strategy, we adopted it in an effort to make the book user-friendly and readable.

This book bears the names of only two authors. However, there were a number of people involved in its development. Our colleague Judith K. Carlson, PhD, offered suggestions and input on several chapters. Valerie Rexin and Katherine Tapscott, students in the Autism Personnel Preparation master's degree program at the University of Kansas, were responsible for developing several examples for Chapter 4 and Chapter 5, respectively. Without the clerical support provided by Ginny Biddulph, this project would never have been brought to fruition. And finally, but in no way of least importance, we thank the parents who contributed information about their lives and their needs, for this was our inspiration.

UNDERSTANDING THE MEANING AND NATURE OF ASPERGER SYNDROME

In 1944, a Viennese psychiatrist by the name of Hans Asperger published a paper describing a social disability, which became known as Asperger Syndrome. In this seminal work, Asperger (1944) described four children with a propensity toward social isolation and awkwardness. In addition to social peculiarities, these children displayed a variety of "typical autistic behaviors" such as self-stimulatory responses and insistence on environmental sameness. Unlike other children with autism, however, they generally had normal intellectual and communication development, leading Asperger to infer that individuals with this disorder represented a distinct and independent diagnostic classification. Over time Asperger made changes in his original conceptualization of children with Asperger Syndrome. However, the essential clinical characteristics remained the same, leading researchers and writers such as Frith (1991) and Wing (1981) to conclude that Asperger's characterizations have withstood the test of time.

Asperger's original paper on autism (1944) and Asperger Syndrome was largely ignored in the United States until recently. Over the past few years, however, Asperger Syndrome has increasingly been recognized by professionals and parents, particularly since the addition of Asperger Syndrome as a subclassification of pervasive developmental disorder in the widely used *Diagnostic and Statistical Manual of Mental Disorders*, Fourth Edition (*DSM-IV*; American Psychiatric Association, 1994). However, understanding of this disability lags significantly behind its recognition.

For example, there is significant debate on whether Asperger Syndrome is an independent diagnostic category or simply another dimension of the so-called "autism spectrum." Indeed, there is enormous disagreement and lack of understanding regarding this disorder and its relationship to other "autistic-like" conditions. This chapter describes characteristics and other issues unique to Asperger Syndrome.

Diagnostic Classification of Asperger Syndrome

Asperger Syndrome has historically been connected with the more widely used term autism. Thus, Kanner's (1943) original description of children with autism (i.e., relationship difficulties, delayed speech and language development and other speech and language abnormalities, normal physical growth and development, insistence on environmental sameness, obsessive preoccupation with objects, and repetitive and other self-stimulatory responses) has served as a general blueprint for understanding individuals with Asperger Syndrome. That is, individuals with Asperger Syndrome have often been thought of as being an upper element of the so-called autism spectrum.

As Kanner's original characteristics of autism have been revised and refined, so too have conceptualizations of Asperger Syndrome. This process of refining the characteristics of Asperger Syndrome was particularly stimulated by Wing (1981), who attempted to clarify and identify the disorder through extensive clinical descriptions and case examples. Others have recently contributed to an increased understanding of Asperger Syndrome, including similarities and differences compared to other autism conditions and diagnostic criteria (Gillberg, 1992; Gillberg & Gillberg, 1989).

The most widely used diagnostic criteria for Asperger Syndrome are included in DSM–IV. This diagnostic and clinical manual classifies Asperger Syndrome as one of five pervasive developmental disorders. According to DSM–IV, pervasive developmental disorders refer to persons who "are characterized by severe and pervasive impairment in several areas of development: reciprocal social interaction skills, communication skills, or the presence of stereotyped behavior, interests, and activities" (p. 65). Other pervasive developmental disorders are identified in DSM–IV: autistic disorder, childhood disintegrative disorder, Rett's disorder, and pervasive development disorder–not otherwise specified. A summary of DSM–IV diagnostic criteria for Asperger Syndrome is shown in Table 1.1.

Description of Children and Youth with Asperger Syndrome

Children and youth with Asperger Syndrome share characteristics with autistic children and youth, as originally described by Kanner (1943), but also have a number of

Table 1.1
DSM–IV Diagnostic Criteria for Asperger Syndrome

A. Qualitative social interaction impairment as shown by at least two of the following:

1. Significant impairment in nonverbal behavior use, including social interaction gestures, facial expression, eye-to-eye contact, and body postures

2. Inability to form developmentally appropriate relationships with peers

3. Failure to spontaneously seek out others for interactions, including sharing interests, enjoyment, or achievements

4. Difficulty with social or emotional reciprocity

B. Repetitive and restricted stereotyped patterns of behavior, activities, and interests, as shown by at least one of the following:

1. Significant preoccupation with one or more stereotyped and restricted interest patterns whose focus or intensity makes it abnormal

2. Significant display of nonfunctional routines or inflexible adherence to rituals

3. Repetitive and stereotyped motor movements such as complex whole-body movements, or hand or finger flapping or twisting

4. Significant and persistent preoccupation with parts of objects

C. Clinically significant social, occupational, or other impairment in functioning

D. Absence of a clinically significant general language delay

E. Absence of a clinically significant delay in cognitive development or in development of age-appropriate adaptive behavior (other than social interaction), self-help skills, and childhood curiosity about the environment

F. Failure to meet diagnostic criteria for schizophrenia or another pervasive developmental disorder

---

unique features. Clinical features of Asperger Syndrome include social interaction impairments, speech and communication characteristics, cognitive and academic characteristics, sensory characteristics, and physical and motor-skill anomalies.

Social Interaction Impairments

Children and youth with Asperger Syndrome demonstrate social deficits and peculiarities that continue into adulthood. Although some children and adolescents appear to be interested in interacting with others, their interactions tend to be inept or characterized by an inability to engage in age-expected social interactions, including appropriate play. Indeed, the social deficits of children and adolescents with

Asperger Syndrome may be due more to a lack of understanding of appropriate social customs than to disinterest or fear of social contact. For example, a child with Asperger Syndrome may appear rude or odd because he is unwilling to take turns in play and conversation or to understand a peer's subtle social cues, in spite of his willingness to seek out others on the playground.

In accordance with these behavioral patterns, children and youth with Asperger Syndrome may be anywhere from withdrawn to active on the behavioral continuum. Regardless of where they fit on this continuum, however, they are routinely viewed as socially awkward, socially stiff, emotionally blunted, self-centered, unable to understand nonverbal social cues, inflexible, and lacking in empathy and understanding. Therefore, even when children and adolescents with Asperger Syndrome actively try to seek out others, they encounter social isolation because of their lack of understanding of the rules of social behavior, including eye contact, proximity to others, gestures, posture, and so forth.

It is not unusual for individuals with Asperger Syndrome to be able to engage in routine social interactions (e.g., greetings) without being able to engage in extended interactions or two-way relationships. Thus, children and youth with Asperger Syndrome are commonly described by families and schoolmates as lacking an awareness of social protocol, lacking common sense, tending to misinterpret social cues and unspoken messages, and being inclined to display a variety of socially unaccepted and nonreciprocal responses.

It is also common for individuals with Asperger Syndrome to become emotionally vulnerable and easily stressed. For example, children with Asperger Syndrome may become agitated if they think others are invading their private space, such as when they are in a crowded room, or when they find themselves in the midst of several simultaneous social activities. However, unlike many normally developing and achieving peers, many children with Asperger Syndrome do not reveal stress through voice tone, body posture, and so forth. As a result, their agitation may escalate to a point of crisis because of others' unawareness of their discomfort along with their own inability to monitor and control uncomfortable situations. Given these deficits, it is not surprising that children and youth with Asperger Syndrome are relatively easy targets for peers prone to teasing and bullying.

In spite of their frequent lack of social awareness, many individuals with Asperger Syndrome are aware that they are different from their peers. Thus, self-esteem problems, self-faultfinding, and self-deprecation are common among individuals with Asperger Syndrome.

Not surprisingly, many individuals with Asperger Syndrome are poor incidental social learners. That is, they tend to learn social skills without fully understanding their meaning and context. Indeed, many of these individuals attempt to rigidly and broadly follow universal social rules, because doing so provides structure to an otherwise confusing world. Unfortunately this is often not a successful strategy because there are few, if any, universal and inflexible social rules. Yet, as any parent or teacher can attest, social relationships are extremely important for persons with Asperger Syndrome, because they facilitate development of self-control, self-knowledge, and use of functional language and related skills needed for day-to-day functioning.

Although behavioral problems are not universal among individuals with Asperger Syndrome, they are not uncommon. These problems often involve feelings of stress, fatigue, or loss of control or inability to predict outcomes. Thus, children with Asperger Syndrome do not have typical conduct problems, but rather behavior problems connected to their inability to function in a world they see as unpredictable and threatening. Thus, it appears that there is little support for Asperger's (1944) original description of children with Asperger Syndrome as malicious and mean-spirited. Rather, when persons with Asperger Syndrome do experience behavioral difficulties, their problems are typically due to social ineptness, an obsessive and single-minded pursuit of a certain interest, or a defensive panic reaction.

Speech and Communication Characteristics

Frith (1991) observed that children with Asperger Syndrome "tend to speak fluently by the time they are five, even if their language development was slow to begin with, and even if their language is noticeably odd in its use for communication" (p. 3). Although professionals generally agree on the course of childhood language development, there are disagreements about the typical time of language onset in children with Asperger Syndrome. Asperger (1944) described language onset as occurring at an expected age, whereas others such as Wing (1981) reported that many individuals with Asperger Syndrome are slow to talk. Wing also reported that many individuals with Asperger Syndrome revealed a variety of communication deficits as infants, and that many of their perceived "special abilities" could be explained as rote responses rather than normal or precocious language development.

Not surprisingly, many children and youth with Asperger Syndrome have good structural language skills, such as clear pronunciation and correct syntax, but poor pragmatic communication abilities. Thus, many of these individuals are poor in using language for social interaction. For example, a child may repeat the same phrase over and over, talk with exaggerated inflections or in a monotone, discuss at length a single topic that is of little interest to others, or have difficulty sustaining conversation unless it focuses on a particular, narrowly defined topic. These communication problems are not surprising, given that effective communication requires that individuals have shared topics and are willing to listen as well as talk. The adult-like and pedantic speaking style of some children with Asperger Syndrome may further lessen their appeal to their peers.

As might be expected, nonverbal communication deficits and related social communication problems are common among persons with Asperger Syndrome. This includes problems during interactions such as standing closer to another person than is customarily accepted; intensely staring at another person for long periods; maintaining abnormal body posture; failing to make eye contact or displaying an inexpressive face, thereby failing to signal interest, approval, or disapproval; and failing to use or understand gestures and facial expressions.

In school, students with Asperger Syndrome frequently have difficulty comprehending descriptions of abstract concepts; understanding and correctly using figures of speech such as metaphors, idioms, parables, and allegories; and grasping the meaning and intent of rhetorical questions. Because these conventions are commonly used by teachers and authors of school texts, deficits in this area have a negative effect on these students' academic success.

Cognitive and Academic Characteristics

Although many students with Asperger Syndrome have average intellectual abilities and are included in general education classrooms, they can be expected to experience some academic performance problems. Indeed, social and communication deficits, in combination with obsessive and narrowly defined interests, concrete and literal thinking styles, inflexibility, poor problem-solving skills, poor organizational skills, difficulty in discerning relevant from irrelevant stimuli, and weak social standing, often make it difficult for students with Asperger Syndrome to fully participate in and comprehend general education curricula and instructional systems. As a result, a number of children and youth with Asperger Syndrome are thought to have learning disabilities (Frith, 1991). In spite of these challenges, children and youth with Asperger Syndrome can go on to college and successful careers.

An additional challenge facing children and youth with Asperger Syndrome relates to their difficulty generalizing knowledge and skills. That is, they frequently have problems applying information and skills across settings and situations and with different individuals. Moreover, it is common for students with Asperger Syndrome to have difficulty attending to relevant curricular cues and stimuli.

Teachers often fail to recognize the special academic needs of students with Asperger Syndrome, because these children often give the impression that they understand more than they do. That is, the deficits of some students with Asperger Syndrome are masked by their pedantic style, seemingly advanced vocabulary, and parrot-like responses, as well as by the fact that they may be good word callers without having the higher order thinking and comprehension skills to understand what they read. Some students with Asperger Syndrome may be compliant and unassertive, which contributes to this problem.

Sensory Characteristics

Both Kanner (1943) and Asperger (1944) shared the observation that children with autism and children with Asperger Syndrome are prone to peculiar sensory stimuli responses. For example, children with Asperger Syndrome are often hypersensitive to certain sounds or visual stimuli, such as fluorescent lights, and may respond negatively when overloaded with certain types of sensory stimuli. In fact, parents and teachers have reported behavior problems associated with these children's fear of anticipated stimuli such as city whistle signals or chimes that are sounded at certain times. It is common for parents of children with Asperger Syndrome to report that these children have an obsessive preference for certain foods or textures (e.g., a child will wear clothes made of only certain fabrics). Some individuals with Asperger Syndrome have been reported to have an extremely high tolerance for physical pain.

Finally, many children with Asperger Syndrome engage in self-stimulatory responses such as repeatedly spinning an object for extended periods of time, engaging in self-stimulatory light filtering, or a number of other aberrant self-stimulatory responses. In fact, DSM–IV (1994) lists "restricted repetitive and stereotyped patterns of behavior, interests, and activities" (p. 77) among the criteria for a diagnosis of Asperger Syndrome. Display of these behaviors is most common when the children experience stress, fatigue, or sensory overload.

Physical and Motor-Skill Anomalies

Wing (1981) observed that children with Asperger Syndrome tend to have poor motor coordination and balance problems. Parents and educators have found that many children and adolescents with Asperger Syndrome are awkward and clumsy, making it difficult for them to successfully participate in games involving motor skills. Because these are primary social activities for children, problems in this area have significant implications for social and pragmatic language development that go well beyond matters of motor coordination. Moreover, fine motor-skill difficulties have implications for a variety of school activities such as writing and art. Although there is some dispute over the existence of motor delays and aberrations among individuals with Asperger Syndrome (Manjiviona & Prior, 1995), there does seem to be sufficient anecdotal evidence to suggest that this is a problem that needs consideration.

Other Features Related to Understanding Asperger Syndrome

Prevalence

The prevalence of Asperger Syndrome has increased in recent years, with current estimates as high as 71 out of every 10,000 births (Gillberg, 1993). Asperger Syndrome is approximately two to three times more common in boys than in girls. Asperger Syndrome has been identified throughout the world among all racial, ethnic, economic, and social groups.

Etiology

The Autism Society of America (1995) contends that autism is the result of a neurological disorder. It also strongly supports the position that there are no known psychological or environmental factors (e.g., "refrigerator mother," parental emotional aloofness, or related interpersonal variables) that cause autism, a position that is shared by virtually every professional associated with the disability. Although causes of Asperger Syndrome are currently unknown, a number of authorities speculate that the disorder shares at least some of the same causal factors as autism (Rumsey, 1992). For example, there appears to be a significant hereditary link for cases of Asperger Syndrome (Frith, 1991).

Prognosis and Outlook

Little is known about the prognosis for persons with Asperger Syndrome. Yet there is every reason to believe that many children and youth with Asperger Syndrome will be able to lead relatively normal lives. Gillberg (1992) has perhaps voiced the most optimistic outlook, noting that "oddities of social style, communication and interests are likely to remain, but the majority of this group hold down jobs and it seems that a large proportion get married and have children" (p. 833). Others have been more guarded about the anticipated course for individuals with Asperger Syndrome (Lord & Venter, 1992; Myles, Simpson, & Becker, 1995). They have observed that the long-term prognosis for individuals with Asperger Syndrome is difficult to determine due to myriad social, symptom, severity, intervention, educational, and other factors associated with the disorder.

In spite of general agreement that the social, communication, and other characteristics associated with Asperger Syndrome are a devastating disability, there is also recognition that with appropriate education, treatment, and support, many of these individuals can lead relatively normal and independent lives (Koegel & Koegel, 1995; Minshew, Goldstein, & Siegel, 1995; Quill, 1995; Waterhouse, Morris, Allen, Dunn, & Fein, 1996).

Case Examples

The following two case examples illustrate the major characteristics of Asperger Syndrome. Although each case is a unique example of Asperger Syndrome, both cases reflect many of the common characteristics of the disability.

JON

Jon is an 8-year-old boy who lives with his 11-year-old sister and his mother, who is a business education teacher at a high school in their community. Jon and his sister also spend several hours each week with their father and his family.

As a baby Jon was perceived to be happy, placid, undemanding, and not prone to cry. His parents reported that he was satisfied to lie in his crib for hours, and that although he would acknowledge their presence, he appeared to have little interest in interacting with others or being held. His parents also reported that unlike his sister, who was assertive in seeking the attention of adults and who talked at an early age, Jon was quiet as a toddler and primarily interested in being by himself, even when around other children. Jon began speaking in single words and short sentences at around 18 months. His parents also noted that he was somewhat delayed, compared to his sister, in walking and developing self-care skills. They were advised by their physician that Jon's delays were mild and thus did not warrant an evaluation.

When Jon was 3 to 4 years old, his parents began to be very concerned about his development. They were particularly alarmed that he would wander around their house aimlessly for hours, his head tilted at an odd angle, holding his earlobes between his thumb and index finger while making a high-pitched, whining noise. They also reported that he would rhythmically parrot commercials he heard on TV (which he would rarely sit and watch), including one advertisement for a detergent product, which the parents found particularly annoying. Their initial response was to ignore these behaviors, based on their belief that their son was slow in developing and that his peculiar behaviors were satisfying some unknown need and thus should be permitted. However, at the urging of relatives, Jon's parents took him to a child psychiatrist when he was 4½. The psychiatrist diagnosed Jon as having pervasive developmental disorder–not otherwise specified and recommended that Jon attend a specialized preschool for at-risk and delayed children and be reevaluated annually.

At a later date the parents reported that they did not like the psychiatrist's demeanor and thus did not seek reevaluation from him. However, they did enroll Jon in a regular preschool supported by their church. Jon attended this program until he was 6, because the parents thought he was unprepared to begin public school. Jon's preschool teachers reported that he was compliant, quiet, and placid. He passively participated in most activities and was not considered a behavior problem. He initiated few interactions with peers, although he would respond to peer initiations. At the age of 6, Jon was enrolled in a regular kindergarten at his neighborhood school. Shortly afterward the parents separated, and they were divorced approximately a year later. The parents reported that the period of separation and divorce was very difficult for their daughter, but that Jon appeared to be oblivious to his father's absence.

Jon currently attends a regular second-grade classroom at a neighborhood elementary school. Jon is eligible for itinerant special education services (his teacher regularly meets with a special education teacher to discuss curriculum adaptations for Jon) and receives weekly, 1-hour, individualized speech–language services; however, his teacher describes him as an "average student." His teacher reports that Jon is slow to complete assignments and often appears confused regarding classroom expectations. However, she notes that once he "catches on" to a task he will obsessively work to complete it. She also notes that he is generally compliant and appears vaguely interested in pleasing her. She also observes that he is extremely orderly in arranging books and other materials in his desk and will sometimes appear overwrought when classroom schedule changes occur. For example, a recent rainstorm required that the children complete their recess in the classroom, a change that appeared to be very hard for Jon to comprehend.

Jon typically stands next to his teacher on the playground, except when he occasionally obsessively wanders the perimeter of the school grounds. Jon is shy and socially isolated from his peers. He will respond briefly when approached by peers; however, he has yet to be observed initiating contact or joining in any games. Jon tends to be very passive, and on more than one occasion he has been bullied by other boys at recess. On these occasions Jon retreats from the aggressor and stands by his teacher.

Jon's mother reports that his behavior of wandering with his head tilted at an odd angle while holding his earlobes and making high-pitched whining noises has decreased significantly over the past year. However, he sometimes obsessively rubs and flaps his hands when he is agitated or stressed.

Approximately a year ago Jon was evaluated at a university child guidance clinic. The mother and father were somewhat disturbed by the diagnosis of Asperger Syndrome. However, after learning more about the condition, they seemed to be willing to accept their son's disability. They seem committed to supporting his continued development.

 TERRY

Terry is 17 and lives with his mother, father, and younger brother. An older sister attends a nearby state university and lives with the family during the summers. The family is middle class, with both parents holding mid-level management positions.

Terry was only recently diagnosed with Asperger Syndrome by a multidisciplinary evaluation team at a children's hospital. Prior to receiving that diagnosis Terry had been identified as learning disabled, "mildly autistic," schizophrenic, and as having a developmental expressive language disorder.

Early records reveal that Terry was slightly delayed in starting to walk and significantly delayed in developing expressive language. He was virtually mute until about age 3, at which time he almost overnight began speaking in long and complicated sentences. In spite of its complexity, however, his language was (and occasionally continues to be) characterized by placing adjectives after the words they describe (e.g., "The car black is coming"). Moreover, he frequently used questions independent of posing an issue (e.g., while standing by himself, Terry mused, "Where are we going to eat dinner with spaghetti on Wednesday; is it in the window room?"). These problems have improved, largely as a result of prompting by parents and teachers. However, Terry's speech remains quite pedantic and limited to a few set topics; his overall communication demeanor is marked by an absence of affect and inflection.

Since he was a young child, Terry has maintained an obsessive interest in toilets and related plumbing equipment. His parents reported that when he was as young as 5 he knew the brand name of the toilets in his home, day care center, father's and mother's businesses, and several of the stores in a nearby shopping center. He also displayed a number of stereotyped repetitive behaviors until he was about 10, including spinning empty 1-liter cola containers and tilting his head and squinting at persons with whom he was standing. He no longer spins cola containers; however, he continues to stare and squint at others with his head tilted.

Terry's family and schoolmates have described him as "odd" since the time he began school. He has never been able to mix with peers, although he daily watches his classmates talk in the hallways between classes. He has occasionally approached classmates; however, his limited repertoire of interests, such as his tendency to describe the plumbing fixtures in the school, has alienated him from his classmates.

According to his parents and teachers, Terry has never had a true friend. In spite of his mother's repeated attempts to arrange relationships with age peers through neighbors and friends and his teachers' development of peer support programs, Terry has remained a loner. Recently, Terry began a program in his special education resource room (where he daily spends 2 hours working on study and vocational skills) in which general education students participate in social activities with special education students. In this program Terry is routinely the one with whom the students least want to interact, even though the other special education students have fewer cognitive, language, and academic abilities and skills. When one regular education classmate was asked about this circumstance, she responded, "He is such a geek—he gets right in my face and only wants to talk about the sinks in the boys' bathroom."

When asked about his future, Terry responds that he wants to be a plumber (an interest his teachers have recently attempted to cultivate to harness his obsessive interest in plumbing fixtures). He also indicates that he wants to marry and be a member of the community Lion's Club. His parents and siblings worry about Terry's future after he completes school, fearing that he will be unprepared to work or live outside the home.

Concluding Thoughts

There is considerable debate regarding whether Asperger Syndrome is an element of the so-called "autism spectrum" or an independent disability unconnected to autism. In spite of this spirited debate, professionals agree that Asperger Syndrome is a serious social and communication disorder that can have devastating effects. However, there is also agreement that the general prognosis for individuals with Asperger Syndrome is relatively good, and that with support and training these individuals can be happy and productive citizens.

CHAPTER

ASSESSING STUDENTS WITH ASPERGER SYNDROME

Authored with Judith K. Carlson

Prescriptive diagnostic assessment is the process of collecting data with the specific purpose of verifying student strengths and concerns. Such data may include a medical history, intelligence and aptitude ratings, academic test scores, and anecdotal records of the student's daily life. Regardless of the source of this data, assessment should focus on academic, behavioral, social, physical, or environmental components (Myles, Constant, Simpson, & Carlson, 1989; Szatmari, 1991). This information is collected to provide the student with appropriate educational placement, to target goals and objectives, to monitor student progress, and to evaluate the quality of the educational services being received. Additionally, multidisciplinary teams may be created to assess across areas such as occupational and physical therapy, audiology, vision, sensory motor therapy, and social work.

Norm-Referenced Assessment

In norm-referenced assessment, standardized tests are used to collect data. Generally, norm-referenced tests use specified questions and administration and scoring procedures. The assumption underlying norm-referenced assessment is that every student receives the same questions and the same administration. The test-taker's performance is compared to the performance of the norm group. A norm group consists of randomly selected students who share certain characteristics.

Items on a norm-referenced test are carefully compiled according to the results of earlier tests conducted with students in the norm group. At the same time, scores on the norm-referenced test are statistically determined by the distribution of scores from the norm group.

Administration of a norm-referenced test is usually specified in detail. If the examiner violates the required administration procedures, the scores obtained in that testing are not valid. Because a norm-referenced test compares the test-taker's performance to that of the norm group, it is necessary to conduct the test in the same way as the norm group experienced it.

Usually, a norm-referenced test yields two or more kinds of scores. First, the student's performance is calculated as a raw score. Next, the raw score is converted to a standard score for comparison with the performance of the norm group. Because the norm group represents the general population from a statistical viewpoint, an examiner can compare a student's performance with that of similar students in the nation.

Norm-Referenced Measures Appropriate for Students with Asperger Syndrome

Many of the more popular norm-referenced tests were created with norm samples that did not contain students with Asperger Syndrome. Thus, examiners must use extra caution when administering and interpreting results of such tests with this population. An examiner should consult the test manual to determine whether the test's norm group is appropriate for the student being assessed. Commonly used norm-referenced tests for students with exceptionalities, including Asperger Syndrome, are categorized into two groups: aptitude/achievement tests and tests of adaptive behavior/social skills.

Aptitude/Achievement Tests

All general intelligence tests can be used with students with Asperger Syndrome. There are advantages and disadvantages of using such tests, depending on the skills and capabilities of the individual student. The *Wechsler Intelligence Scale for Children–Third Edition* (WISC–III; Wechsler, 1991) and the *Stanford-Binet Intelligence Scale–Fourth Edition* (Thorndike, Hagen, & Sattler, 1985) are widely used intelligence tests in the fields of education and psychology. Standardized scores yielded by most other norm-referenced tests are comparable with scores of these two intelligence tests.

It is important to note that no students with Asperger Syndrome were identified in the norm groups for these two tests. It is possible to substitute other standardized measures that may more directly access the abilities of students with Asperger Syndrome.

Tests of Adaptive Behavior/Social Skills

Adaptive behavior and social skills are common deficits for students with Asperger Syndrome (Wing, 1991). The *Vineland Adaptive Behavior Scale* (VABS; Sparrow, Balla, & Cicchetti, 1984) is frequently used to examine behavioral and social skills of children with Asperger Syndrome. There are three independent forms of the VABS. Two of the forms, the Expanded Form and the Survey Form, are administered by interviewing the student's primary caregiver. The third form is the Classroom Edition, which is conducted with a teacher. All three forms assess the domains of communication, daily living, socialization, and motor skills. The Expanded Form and the Survey Form also assess a maladaptive behavior domain.

One concern about the VABS is that it is not scored by direct observation of the student (Parks, 1988). However, administration of the VABS is relatively easy, and it yields a reliable standard score that can be compared with other norm-referenced tests.

Informal Assessment

Informal assessment refers to a practitioner's collecting, evaluating, and applying information about a student. The data obtained through informal assessment are frequently used to set goals, identify instructional strategies, and measure outcome behaviors (Guerin & Maier, 1983). Informal assessment procedures target what the student knows and how the student learns, allowing practitioners to select instructional techniques that facilitate learning.

Informal assessment does not require a reference group against which to measure student performance. Rather, students are compared to their own performance levels within the curriculum and the demands of the program or placement. Therefore, data can be collected in a variety of settings: classroom, home, workplace, clinic, or testing facility. Information obtained through informal assessment frequently involves ordinary classroom interactions and may be idiosyncratic (Guerin & Maier, 1983).

The physical environment, task presentation, level of interest, and past learning experience can all influence how well a person with Asperger Syndrome performs on a test. Informal assessment requires no rigid time constraints or standardized procedures. As a result, students with Asperger Syndrome can approach problem solving in traditional or nontraditional ways. Because no time limit is specified, the examiner can start and progress as he or she becomes familiar with the student, allowing time to build rapport.

Designing an assessment to elicit certain behaviors can also provide important information. For example, is the student able to ask for help or indicate that he or she would like to take a break from the test? If not, how does the student communicate needs? Understanding a student's functioning level can lead to an understanding of how the student approaches tasks and indicates readiness skills in academics or social development. This information can aid in establishing realistic goals that are crucial for encouraging learning and building success. Setting multiple goals—those that the student can readily accomplish, those that are more difficult, and those that are challenging, yet motivating—helps to create a best-practices intervention program. Throughout testing, the examiner should identify which tasks are easy or difficult for the student and note which activities, materials, and methods receive the most positive response.

Although it can be used as a part of a full evaluation battery, informal assessment is best suited for data collection that is ongoing and fluid. Revising individualized education plan (IEP) objectives, selecting instruction and response formats, modifying assignments, setting time frames for performance, and developing individualized curriculum can all be enhanced using informal assessment data.

Areas of Consideration

Myles et al. (1989) listed major areas of consideration for using informal assessment with students with Asperger Syndrome. These areas include (a) stimulus overselectivity, (b) motivation, and (c) self-stimulatory behavior.

Stimulus Overselectivity

Stimulus overselectivity occurs when a student eliminates all but a few cues in the environment. For example, when shown word cards with the verbal instruction "Point to the card with the word *exit* on it," the student may continually select the card on the left. This response pattern can easily be disrupted by varying the presentation of the task, the arrangement of the stimuli, or the manner in which the examiner requests the information.

Motivation

Limited motivation can be confused with an inability to complete a task or a lack of interest in the task. Students with Asperger Syndrome frequently require external motivation to complete a task. Prior to testing, it is important to determine appropriate reinforcers, break times, and preferred tasks. Talking with parents, teachers, caregivers, and the student can provide several reinforcers to combat limited motivation. Such reinforcers as tangible objects, picture boards, or simple tokens can motivate the student to complete the task.

Self-Stimulatory Behaviors

Many students with Asperger Syndrome exhibit self-stimulatory behaviors such as hand flapping or light filtering. If these repetitive movements are not interfering with test administration or response, they should be ignored during the assessment. If the self-stimulatory behaviors are disruptive, however, it may be necessary to work with the student to achieve appropriate response behaviors. Regardless, anecdotal records regarding the student's self-stimulatory behaviors should be maintained, as they can provide valuable information about the student's frustration levels and coping mechanisms.

Academic Areas

Evaluation of the student with Asperger Syndrome must include the three major academic areas: reading, mathematics, and oral and written language. An assessment that encompasses these areas will provide information for use in instruction.

Assessment of each of these areas can include commercial tests, a "scope-and-sequence" approach, or the school's own curriculum. Commercial items are beneficial because they usually take little time to prepare and often apply to a wide range of skills. Examples of commercial tests are the *Hudson Educational Skills Inventory* (HESI; Hudson, Colson, & Welch, 1989) and the *Brigance Diagnostic Inventory of Essential Skills* (Brigance, 1980).

With a scope-and-sequence approach, a skill or concept is broken down into its component parts. The first component is taught and practiced until it is mastered. Then, the next component is taught, and so on. A scope and sequence can be developed for most academic, functional, behavioral, social, and vocational areas. A scope-and-sequence approach is invaluable for students with Asperger Syndrome, especially when they have splinter skills. A student has a splinter skill if he or she can complete a specific step of a task, yet may not possess the ability to complete prior or subsequent steps. For example, a student may be able to recite the numbers 1 through 200, yet not be able to understand the concept of one-to-one correspondence. Looking at a math scope and sequence will show where rote counting falls on a continuum of math skills and what skills lie between understanding the concept of one-to-one correspondence and counting numbers up to 200. Consideration should be given to the individual student's learning preferences when selecting a scope-and-sequence approach for assessment or intervention. Students who favor a simultaneous or "big picture" approach do not perform well with a scope-and-sequence approach.

Curriculum-based assessments are advantageous for most students because items are drawn from the school's curriculum. Students are assessed on skills that are taught in school, in the order that they are presented. The major disadvantage of this type of assessment is the time that it takes to develop an assessment protocol. A secondary disadvantage is the focus of the assessment. That is, emphasis is typically placed on whether or not the student can perform a task, not on how the student approaches the task. The latter, of course, has great instructional implications. Similar to the scope-and-sequence approach, splinter skills and student learning preferences must be considered.

Reading

Reading is a complex area to assess, as many of the subskills are interrelated. For students with Asperger Syndrome, the major consideration should be comprehension. Although many students with Asperger Syndrome may exhibit solid mechanical reading skills (i.e., appropriate decoding and sight vocabulary skills), their understanding of passages and their ability to relate that understanding to everyday experience may be limited. As students progress through the educational system, mechanical abilities become less important while understanding and generalization become more critical. Thus, reading assessment of children and youth with Asperger Syndrome must emphasize comprehension and application.

A composite of specialized subareas must be developed, resulting in an individualized and integrated reading assessment plan for each student. Two basic reading levels must be established. First is the student's *independent reading level,* that level at which the student can read with 98–100% word accuracy and demonstrate comprehension of 90–100%. Second is the student's *instructional reading level,* that level at which the student can recognize words with 95% accuracy and demonstrate comprehension of 75% or higher. These data must be determined both orally and silently.

This information can be gained through a curriculum-based assessment or through a commercial informal reading inventory, such as the *Classroom Reading Inventory* (Silvaroli, 1986) or the *Durrell Analysis of Reading Difficulty* (Durrell & Catterson, 1981).

It is important to select comprehension questions that will evaluate both recognition and recall response levels. Students with Asperger Syndrome may be able to answer general information questions without understanding the information on a concrete level; hence, it is necessary to develop questions that address a variety of comprehension levels. In addition to factual and vocabulary questions (part of most commercial informal reading inventories), inferential and main idea questions must also be included, along with assessment of the ability to predict outcome, draw conclusions, and distinguish fact from fantasy.

The ability to sequence visual materials is a necessary prerequisite for more complex comprehension; consequently, any student who has difficulty with passage comprehension should be assessed in this area. This ability can be assessed with a series of three or more picture cards (the more cards, the more complex the process) that describe the steps of an activity. Commercial sequencing cards can be used; however, if a student has difficulty responding to such materials, the examiner can make an informal series of cards based on a common activity that is familiar to the student (e.g., brushing teeth).

A miscue analysis should be performed on oral reading passages at the student's instructional level. This involves examining the pattern of errors in the passages, emphasizing such qualities as the incorrect word's graphic similarity to the printed word, the occurrence of interclass (e.g., noun for verb) and intraclass (e.g., noun for noun) substitutions, and percentage of self-corrections. Such analysis supplements the traditional error marking recommended in many informal reading inventories (i.e., those focusing on differentiating substitutions, omissions, deletions, and repetitions). Miscue analysis may give insight into the student's reading skills as a total process, including use of context, logic cues, word recognition, and analysis.

The student's listening capacity should also be assessed. This is the level at which students comprehend material read aloud. The examiner reads passages, starting one grade level above a student's established instructional reading level and continuing until a student demonstrates less than 75% comprehension. Although it is common for normally achieving learners to exhibit a higher capacity for listening than for oral or silent reading, this may not be the case for the student with Asperger Syndrome.

The student's contextual analysis strengths and weaknesses may be determined by using a cloze procedure. This involves taking a reading passage of approximately 250 words at the student's instructional level and systematically deleting every seventh or ninth word. The first and last sentences of the passage remain intact. The student then silently reads the passage, filling in the blanks based on the context. Intraclass substitutions that make sense in context should be accepted as correct. Analysis focuses on the types of cues (e.g., surrounding words, pictures, bold or italic print, or the general story plot) used to interpret the material.

The student's response to certain teaching techniques, such as language experience approach or morphographic or multisensory reading, can also be examined as a part of the assessment process. For example, to analyze the effectiveness of the language experience approach, the student creates and dictates a story to the examiner. Different stimuli such as pictures, open-ended sentences, and activities can be used for story development. The examiner then selects words from the story, writes them on flash cards, and practices with the student. Finally, the complete story is read, first in a choral format (examiner and student reading aloud simultaneously) and then independently by the student. The examiner compares the student's reading abilities using the self-generated stories and published reading materials.

With comprehension as the major assessment focus for students with Asperger Syndrome, the remaining areas in a traditional reading assessment battery (word analysis and word recognition) may carry little importance, as it is possible that students with Asperger Syndrome may have adequate analysis and recognition skills. However, when additional information is desired, further assessment may be used.

A phonics measure can be used to determine specific phonetic components students use in word analysis (decoding). Most commercial phonics measures are based on the formation of nonsense words, thus isolating consonants, vowels, blends, digraphs, and diphthongs. Two factors must be considered when determining the need to administer a phonics measure. First, for students in mainstream educational settings, phonics training traditionally ends during the early elementary years. Accordingly, phonics instruction is usually recommended only in cases where a student has already acquired and demonstrated the majority of basic phonics skills, thus allowing for training in specific skill areas. The second factor relates to the application of phonetic skills in reading. Some students may exhibit an overreliance on phonics, without regard to non–rule-based pronunciations or contextual clues.

Table 2.1
Diagnostic Sequence in Reading

Sequence for older elementary children

A. Informal reading inventory (silent and oral)

    1. Curriculum-based

    2. Commercial

B. Miscue analysis

C. Levels of comprehension (recognition and recall)

    1. Factual

    2. Inferential

    3. Main idea

    4. Predicting outcomes

    5. Drawing conclusions

    6. Fact vs. fantasy

    7. Vocabulary

    8. Sequencing

D. Listening capacity

E. Cloze procedures

F. Fluency and rate

Sequence for younger elementary children

A. Informal reading inventory (silent and oral)

    1. Curriculum-based

    2. Commercial

B. Miscue analysis

C. Levels of comprehension (recognition and recall)

    1. Factual

    2. Inferential

    3. Main idea

    4. Predicting outcomes

(continues)

Table 2.1 *Continued.*

---

5. Drawing conclusions

6. Fact vs. fantasy

7. Vocabulary

8. Sequencing

D. Listening capacity

E. Phonics (in isolation and within words)

F. Sight words (flash and analysis)

G. Alphabet recognition (particulary if low phonics or sight words)

H. Language experience

1. Reads own written stories

2. Reads own words on flash cards

3. Comprehends own stories (recognition and recall)

I. Sequencing of visual material and relating story

Word recognition is assessed by determining the student's sight word vocabulary. This may take several directions, depending on the student's age and reading skills. Core word lists such as those by Dolch (1955) or Fry (1980) can be used to identify words students should know by sight by grade level. These lists are particularly useful with younger students who have limited reading vocabularies or who are in inclusive environments. For older students who exhibit limited vocabulary, sight word lists stressing survival words (e.g., Brigance, 1980) should be included in the assessment package. Table 2.1 provides an overview of the diagnostic sequence in reading.

Mathematics

Mathematics is typically considered a hierarchical subject. That is, if early skills are not established, further skills cannot be mastered (Mercer, 1996). Each skill is thought of in terms of components because many mathematic skills include a number of components.

This traditional approach to mathematics applies to the student with Asperger Syndrome. The student with Asperger Syndrome may have computation skills without having prerequisite readiness skills. For example, the student with splinter skills (e.g., computation skills in the absence of numerical understanding) has not mastered a meaningful task. Instead, the student has memorized a rote skill, which serves little functional purpose. The skill holds no meaning for the student; it cannot be applied to any simulated or real-life setting. Thus, mathematics must be considered a hierarchical subject for students with Asperger Syndrome, and assessment of this area must proceed sequentially. Specific attention should be paid to basic concepts, computation, problem solving, and functional skills.

Basic concepts assessment determines whether students with Asperger Syndrome have mastered skills basic to the understanding of mathematics. According to Piaget (1959) and Mercer (1996), these skills include the following:

1. classification—the ability to judge similarities and differences by color, shape, size, or function

2. number conservation—the ability to deduce that amounts remain the same even when appearances change (e.g., the amount of water in two different containers is equal)

3. ordering and seriation—the ability to arrange items without considering the quantitative relationship between them or to arrange items based on a change in a property (e.g., arranging items of various lengths from shortest to longest)

4. one-to-one correspondence—the ability to understand that one object in a set is the same number as one object in another set, regardless of characteristics (e.g., six apples represent the same quantity as six buttons)

These skills should be assessed systematically at the concrete, semi-concrete, and abstract levels.

Computation involves the calculation of an equation. This basic mathematics area may be a strength for students with Asperger Syndrome. That is, these students may be able to answer problems correctly without understanding the process underlying the calculation. A test that probes comprehension of the proper algorithm, or computational method, is the *Clinical Math Interview* (CMI; Skrtic, Kvam, & Beals, 1983). After working designated problems, a student with Asperger Syndrome explains in an interview format how problems were solved. CMI administration reveals (a) a student's current level of arithmetic functioning, (b) how a student works a problem, and (c) whether a student is dependent on incorrect algorithms. Analysis of computation errors can reveal information about a student's mathematical skills in four categories:

1. wrong operation—the student performs an operation other than the one that is required to solve the problem

2. computational error—the student applies the correct operation, but the response is based on errors in recalling number facts

3. defective algorithm—the student applies the correct operation but makes errors other than fact

4. random response—the student's response shows no discernible relationship to the problem (Roberts, 1968)

Problem solving is the ability to use computational skills meaningfully to solve word or story problems. According to Reisman (1972), a problem is used to initiate this type of learning. Problem solving is dependent on knowledge and application of basic concepts, computation, and generalization. Problem-solving assessment must consider a student's ability to (a) identify important features in a problem-solving situation, (b) translate a verbal sentence into a mathematical sentence, and (c) calculate a solution. Assessment must reveal a student's competence at each level of problem solving. Students with Asperger Syndrome typically demonstrate difficulty with the non-rote skills, such as identifying important problem-solving features and translating a verbal sentence into a mathematical sentence.

Functional skills assessment involves the use of computational and problem-solving skills to respond to real-life situations. Functional skills include time, money, measurement, and geometry. These are particularly important to students with Asperger Syndrome, because they are potential life skills. In fact, the goal of instruction in the other mathematical areas (i.e., basic skills, computation, problem solving) should be to assist students with Asperger Syndrome in successfully using functional skills. Thus, assessment of these skills is extremely important. Table 2.2 provides an overview of the diagnostic sequence in mathematics.

Oral and Written Language

Because students with Asperger Syndrome often have a variety of unique language characteristics (e.g., perseveration, idiosyncratic language), assessment of oral and written language may present particular problems. Unfortunately, oral language is not an area most educators are trained to address; therefore, they tend to refer children with problems in this area to a speech–language pathologist (Moran, 1982). Such a thorough diagnostic work-up may be helpful, but it usually does not address all pertinent classroom-related skills, activities, and issues. Although language acquisition follows a developmental sequence, it is not as clearly hierarchical as math and thus requires a different assessment approach. Because the ability to communicate is partially dependent upon the environment, it is necessary to examine a student's language in a variety of settings and conditions to form an adequate picture of his or her language skills and to determine appropriate areas for intervention.

Normally developing and achieving students provide teachers with numerous spontaneous language samples that allow for assessment in natural settings. They tell stories, converse on the playground, and engage in role playing. These samples can be tape-recorded for subsequent transcription and analysis. To produce stories or conversations for analysis, students with Asperger Syndrome, on the other hand, may need additional encouragement, stimulus, or pre-planning. For example, a special occasion, such as a field trip or a movie, may be used as a topic of discussion. Also,

Table 2.2
Diagnostic Sequence in Mathematics

Sequence for older elementary children

A. Overview of skills

    1. Number/notation

    2. Mathematical language

    3. Ordinality

    4. Place value

    5. Geometric concepts

    6. Fractions

    7. Measurement

    8. Mathematical applications

    9. Word problems

    10. Estimation

    11. Graphing

B. Probes based on difficulties with overview skills

C. Informal math inventory

D. Error pattern analysis

E. *Clinical Math Interview* (CMI)

Sequence for younger elementary children

A. Overview of skills based on Piaget's levels (concrete, semi-concrete, abstract)

    1. Numeration

    2. Mathematical language

    3. Measurement

    4. Place value

    5. One-to-one correspondence

    6. Geometry

    7. Computation

    8. Fractions

(continues)

Table 2.2 *Continued.*

9. Conservation of sets

10. Graphing

B. Probes based on difficulties with overview skills

C. Word problems presented orally

D. Math facts presentation (flash and analysis)

with some students with Asperger Syndrome, a picture or topic may be used to produce a sample.

Written language samples can be elicited in much the same way, that is, by asking a student to tell a story in writing, with or without prompts. However, examiners must keep in mind the motor skills of a student with Asperger Syndrome. If the student has motor problems, two written samples may be gathered: one written by hand and one generated on a computer.

Oral and written language samples may be analyzed and compared on a number of variables. Because oral language generally precedes written language, it is reasonable to expect that most students' oral samples will be more complex than their written work. Thus, oral abilities are most often analyzed to determine initial instructional priorities and to group students for language instruction. If teachers wish to compare a student's language development to that of his or her peers, parallel samples may be taken from an average student of the same age and sex. Many of the elements considered in language assessment are subjective; therefore, care should be taken to consider language samples in the context of both the current environment and the child's cultural background. Language differences due to ethnic background should not be confused with language problems. These have different instructional implications (Johnson, 1996).

An initial area of language assessment is communicative content, which focuses on answering the following questions: What type of story did the student relate? Did it have a beginning, middle, and end? Was it coherent? Was it interesting and creative?

Complexity of language should also be considered. Such assessment examines the proportion of simple, compound, and complex sentences. In written language, this analysis focuses on what a student intended rather than on punctuation. For instance: Does the student use only one sentence type or demonstrate ability to use a variety of simple and complex forms? Is there a difference between oral and written sentence length and complexity? Does the student use an effective descriptive vocabulary? Does the student use colorful adjectives and phrases or choose simple words that can be correctly applied and spelled with confidence? Does the student possess a vocabulary adequate to communicate his or her intent?

Grammar is a third area for language analysis and comparison. It includes most of the features of language generally taught in English classes, including subject-verb agreement, pronoun usage, correct usage of word endings to indicate verb tense, plurals, and possessives. As in other areas of assessment, an effort should be made to distinguish between environmental or cultural differences in language and the student's lack of a specific language skill.

Transcription skills are an additional written language consideration. Specifically, this includes appropriate use of capital letters, punctuation, spelling, and handwriting. Spelling errors are analyzed as to type (i.e., whether misspelled words are rule-based, predictable, or unpredictable).

Additional issues related to understanding language in context may need to be examined in students with language-related learning problems. Some of these students are extremely literal, acknowledging only one meaning for a word. Other students with Asperger Syndrome have not developed a schema or framework that enables them to relate new words to words already in their vocabulary. A simple way to assess these problems is to devise activities that assess knowledge of common idioms or proverbs (e.g., ask the student to explain "Don't cry over spilt milk.") or that check understanding of categorical grouping (e.g., "How do these things go together—fork, knife, and spoon?"). Understanding of synonyms and antonyms may be assessed in a similar manner.

A final language area to examine is the student's knowledge of school vocabulary, that is, those words that frequently appear in oral and written directions or that are necessary to understand particular subject matter (e.g., in math, "calculate," "solve," "determine"). If a student cannot understand the vocabulary used to convey instructions or deliver content, appropriate responses cannot be expected. Table 2.3 provides an overview of the diagnostic sequence in oral and written language.

Student Learning Traits

A student's achievement is influenced by a variety of factors. External factors, such as the bus ride to school or where the student's desk is located in the classroom, have an impact that is easy to recognize and observe. Internal factors, such as how students perceive or receive information, how they process and store concepts, and how they apply these data to their daily lives are more elusive; however, this type of variable must be measured subjectively, through direct observation of the student, examination of classroom materials and setting demands, and pinpointing of instructional and response preferences. These indicators of how children learn are called *student learning traits* (SLT).

According to Myles et al. (1989), student learning traits offer insight into how students with Asperger Syndrome gain information across academic areas. For example, a student may respond to only meaningful stimuli and not to rote stimuli. Some students may be sequential learners, preferring tasks presented in a part-to-whole format,

Table 2.3
Diagnostic Sequence in Oral and Written Language

Sequence for older elementary children

A. Oral language sample (with and without brainstorming)

B. Written language sample (with and without brainstorming)

C. Spelling of known words (looking for organization)

    1. Rule-based

    2. Predictable and unpredictable words

    3. Retest words missed in writing in oral mode

    4. Retest words missed at recall level using recognition level

    5. Retest words missed at recognition level using proofing format

D. Capitalization and punctuation (in contrived sample)

E. Following multistep directions (in written and oral modes)

F. Idioms, synonyms, antonyms, categories

G. Academic language in content areas

H. Near/far point copying

Sequence for younger elementary children

A. Oral language sample (with different stimuli)

B. Language experience story

C. Sequencing

D. Written language sample (one sentence from story or story creation)

E. Writing alphabet (from memory or from model if reversals appear)

F. Personal information (name, address, telephone number)

G. Spelling of known words

    1. Retest words missed in writing in oral mode

    2. Retest words missed at recall level using recognition level

    3. Retest words missed at recognition level using proofing format

H. Following multistep directions (in written and oral modes)

I. Idioms, synonyms, antonyms, categories

J. Academic language in content areas

K. Near/far point copying

whereas others may favor a simultaneous, "big picture" approach. There are as many learning traits as there are students, and each student possesses specific traits. Student learning traits have been divided into three basic categories: learning and memory, behavioral patterns and characteristics, and strategies.

Learning and Memory

Learning and memory refer to those skills that allow students to focus their attention and store information. Sequential versus simultaneous processing, stimulus selectivity, and attention to detail are all in this category. A student's memory skills, including short-term, long-term, visual, auditory, rote, and meaningful memory, play a role in creating the individual's learning style. Tasks that examine students' preferences and strengths within these areas can be contrived and observed for the purpose of shaping instruction.

A student's rate of performance and task pacing also contribute to learning style. Take, for example, the case of Trudy, a young woman with Asperger Syndrome who was being served in a residential treatment center for adolescents with severe behavioral problems. Trudy was thought to be stubborn and oppositional by her house staff, teachers, and therapists because she rarely answered questions or offered input during school and therapy sessions. An examination of Trudy's learning style revealed that she needed a wait time of 20 to 30 seconds to access and process information, rather than the traditional 3- to 5-second wait time experienced in reciprocal conversation. When given adequate wait time, Trudy was able to offer insights and actively participate in her program goals.

Incidental learning, independent work habits, and generalization skills round out this category of student learning traits.

Behavioral Patterns and Characteristics

How students act on environmental stimuli and retrieved information and the unique way they apply this information to daily functioning reveal their behavioral patterns and characteristics. All types of interactional patterns are observed, including adult-to-student, student-to-peer, and small- and large-group interchanges. The student's pattern of response to reinforcement, structure, stress, and success should also be examined. Further, avoidance behaviors, attention-seeking behaviors, and self-stimulatory patterns are all part of a student's behavioral profile. Through structured observation of the student in a variety of settings, the examiner can note on-task and off-task characteristics, flexibility in moving from one activity to the next, and the type of events that trigger impulsive or compulsive behavior.

For students with Asperger Syndrome, some specific behavioral patterns must be considered. The use of echolalia as a communication tool, the ability to make and maintain eye contact, and the level of distractibility and perseverance are all important links to successful classroom performance. Eye, hand, and foot dominance, as well as the ability to cross midline, must also be examined to determine perceptual abilities and fine- and gross-motor skills. These areas can easily be tapped by having the student visually track a favorite toy, catch and kick a ball, and draw or write. Midline issues can be addressed by having the student complete a simple shape or interlocking puzzle. The examiner places puzzle pieces on opposite sides of the puzzle board and observes whether the student reaches across himself or herself to place the puzzle pieces. Any patterns of oral or written perseveration should also be noted. Of course, the important issue in examining any behavioral pattern or characteristic is determining which behaviors affect the student's interactions with academic requirements and social skills.

Strategies

Strategies are the techniques or rules that a student uses to solve problems and independently complete tasks. It is important to determine what types of strategies a student uses and whether the student can learn or develop new strategies. Sometimes a student may approach tasks very strategically yet elect to use strategies that are ineffective or inappropriate. Students with Asperger Syndrome frequently persist in using unsuccessful strategies simply because they know no replacement strategies for the given situation.

Following written and oral directions is another important strategic thinking component. Many students with Asperger Syndrome are unable to organize or prioritize multilevel instructions and require brief, small instructional steps for successful task completion.

It is also important to consider the types of metacognitive strategies that a student applies. Metacognitive strategies include skills such as self-talk, self-monitoring, and self-correction. For example, a young child who is helping her parent make lunch for her family may use a metacognitive strategy. As she makes sandwiches, she may verbally direct herself by saying, "First I spread the peanut butter on the bread and then I get out the jelly." Children with Asperger Syndrome may never have rehearsed these typical developmental activities, and therefore must experience them through direct instructional procedures. Table 2.4 provides a noninclusive list of sample student learning traits.

Levels of Skill Acquisition

Levels of skill acquisition must be considered when planning the assessment of a student with Asperger Syndrome. Specifically, assessment should occur at the following levels of acquisition: recognition, recall, and application. These levels, which were adapted from instructional levels of presentation (Hudson, Colson, & Braxdale, 1984), are hierarchical, with recognition representing the lowest level of acquisition and application the highest level. If an examiner can determine at which level a student has demonstrated skill mastery, instruction can be appropriately planned.

Table 2.4
Student Learning Traits

I. Learning and Memory

How students approach instruction by focusing their attention and storing information. How complex a pattern can the student perform?

A. Sequential learner

B. Simultaneous learner

C. Stimulus selectivity

D. Attention to detail

E. Memory skills

  1. Short-term

  2. Long-term

  3. Visual

  4. Auditory

  5. Rote

  6. Meaningful

F. Pacing

G. Performance rate

H. Incidental learning

I. Independent work habits

J. Generalization

II. Strategies

Techniques, principles, or rules that allow students to complete tasks independently and successfully solve problems. How are novel tasks approached? How does the student solve problems already known? How does the student organize information?

A. Strategic learner

B. Memory strategies

C. Problem-solving strategies

  1. Academic

  2. Social

D. Metacognitive strategies

  1. Organizational

  2. Self-talk

(continues)

Table 2.4 *Continued.*

---

    3. Self-monitoring

    4. Self-correction

  E. Following oral directions

  F. Following written directions

III. Behavioral Patterns and Characteristics

How students apply retrieved information to daily functioning. Which behaviors affect interactions with academic requirements and social skills?

  A. Group interactions

  B. Peer relationships

  C. Adult relationships

  D. Avoidance behaviors

  E. Attention-seeking behaviors

  F. Self-stimulatory behaviors

  G. Response to reinforcement

  H. Response to structure

  I. Response to stressors

  J. Response to success

  K. On-task and off-task behavior

  L. Flexibility or inflexibility

  M. Impulsive behavior

  N. Compulsive behavior

  O. Echolalia

  P. Perseveration (oral, motor, or written)

  Q. Dominance

  R. Perseverance

  S. Distractibility

  T. Eye contact

  U. Excessive movement

  V. Sense of humor

  W. Self-concept

To assess the recognition level, an examiner might ask a student with Asperger Syndrome to select a stimulus item from similar distractors. At this level of skill acquisition, the student is not expected to generate the correct response without cues, but is expected only to discriminate an item from similar stimuli through a written or oral response. Assessment activities at the recognition level include multiple-choice or matching items. These activities allow students to respond through pointing, underlining, circling, or matching appropriate items. Students who successfully perform recognition-level tasks typically demonstrate readiness to generate original thought relative to that task.

Assessment at the recall level involves asking students to retrieve information or perform tasks without stimulus clues. At this level, students generate thoughts, ideas, or concepts, responding orally or in writing to assessment items. Activities that assess skill acquisition at the recall level include fill-in-the-blank, flash card, or short-answer items. The student who successfully completes a task at the recall level is prepared to apply rote information in a more meaningful manner.

The application level of skill acquisition represents the meaningful use of a skill in a simulated or contrived setting. Assessment tasks are structured so that students can demonstrate proficiency in the classroom or other setting. The importance of application-level assessment was seen in the movie *Rainman*. In this movie, Raymond Babbitt, a man with autism played by Dustin Hoffman, demonstrated a unique ability with numbers. He could perform recall-level tasks in mathematics, specifically, adding, subtracting, multiplying, and dividing large numbers without the aid of a calculator or response cues. However, when asked to apply numerical skills to a real-life setting (i.e., use numbers to indicate an understanding of money), his lack of application skills was evident. Assessment tasks at the application level include word problems, theme writing, and comprehending and following written directions.

Levels of Instructional Representation

Many of the current practices in cognitive development and education are based upon the developmental theories of Jean Piaget (1959). From Piaget's description of the type of knowledge displayed by children at various stages of development from birth to adulthood, Bruner (1966) specified three levels of representation through which a child must progress to become an independent learner. The first stage is the *concrete*, or enactive, during which the student is actively and physically involved in a learning task. Many children learn best by "doing," whether learning to ride a bicycle or learning the concept of place value in math. In either case, the student interacts with a physical object—the bicycle or place-value manipulatives (e.g., blocks)— to gain a concrete understanding of the process. At this level, the student develops a schema that becomes the basis for future knowledge.

The second, or *iconic*, stage involves the use of graphics or images to prompt the student to retrieve the prior knowledge needed to complete a task or solve a problem.

A common iconic instructional presentation is the use of pictures or diagrams in math. Most students who used blocks to grasp the concept of place value should be able to respond to items illustrated with drawings of blocks. Bruner (1966) described this stage as governed by principles of perceptual organization.

Symbolic, the final stage, involves representation in language or words. Students at this level of representation have developed a schema, or pattern, based on past experiences with a task and are able to respond appropriately to symbols (e.g., words) on a page without further prompts or clues. For instance, a student given a math problem involving regrouping for addition or subtraction will recall his prior experience with place value and apply that knowledge to computing the answer.

Normal development proceeds sequentially through the three stages; however, students with Asperger Syndrome may have gaps in their knowledge, resulting in splinter skills. For example, they may have developed the ability to work with abstract symbols without understanding the underlying concepts or being able to work with concrete manipulatives.

When assessing students with Asperger Syndrome for purposes of instructional planning, examiners should determine whether students are able to demonstrate comprehension on all three levels: concrete, iconic, and symbolic. Examiners must assess students' understanding of underlying concepts, as well as their ability to respond to written problems at an abstract level. Students who have a great deal of rote knowledge or who have developed a successful strategy for test taking may do relatively well on written tests but be deficient in concrete, conceptual understanding needed to build a solid academic knowledge base. Accordingly, teachers and diagnosticians should schedule at least some assessment at the concrete and iconic levels, areas typically not examined beyond the primary grades.

Diagnostic Teaching

As with student learning traits, the focus of diagnostic teaching is listening to the student, understanding what he or she feels, and interpreting the subsequent interactions within the learning environment. It is a systematic, clinical process in which the student is presented with a task or series of tasks that are new. The student is asked to solve a problem or complete an activity while the examiner notes observations and maintains anecdotal records. These notes should describe how the student approaches the task, deals with task frustration, and modifies and self-corrects errors, as well as what problem-solving skills the student uses while completing the task. As the diagnostic teaching session progresses, the examiner may offer clues or suggestions and even teach small components needed to complete the task.

Another application of diagnostic teaching involves presenting similar tasks to the student using a variety of presentation and/or response modes. For example, six spelling words, all unfamiliar to the student and similar in structure and difficulty, are presented for practice using three different modalities. The student practices two words verbally by spelling the word aloud and then using the word in a sentence. The student practices another two words in a written format by writing each word 10 times. The student practices the final two words kinesthetically by drawing the letters in a box of damp sand. Each practice session lasts approximately 3 minutes. At the conclusion of the practice sessions, the student is tested, through the same type of response required in his or her classroom. The results are then compared to see if different practice modes facilitated the student's memorization of the spelling words. Common presentation and response modes used in this type of diagnostic teaching include visual, auditory, tactile or kinesthetic, and combinations of two or more of these modalities.

Diagnostic teaching sessions are usually brief, lasting 15 minutes or less. Throughout the session, the examiner observes the student's response patterns and notes areas of strength. The practitioner works with the student's strengths, addresses deficit skill areas, introduces compensatory mechanisms, and rearranges home and school environments to meet the student's specific learning needs.

Portfolio Analysis

Recent changes in assessment have led from a reliance on formal tests to a more person-centered approach (Nolet, 1992; Schutt & McCabe, 1994; Wesson & King, 1992). Practitioners are acknowledging that one-shot assessments may not reveal the small or idiosyncratic gains made by students with developmental disabilities. Portfolio assessment, which recognizes small changes in performance, can yield valuable prescriptive information (Hendrick-Keefe, 1995). Portfolio assessment requires students to evaluate their current level of functioning in a specific area while simultaneously requiring the instructor to review educational programming to ensure that goals directly address the students' needs (Schutt & McCabe). Therefore, portfolio assessment promotes accountability for both student and instructor. Portfolios provide a full picture of a student's abilities by concentrating on strengths and gains rather than on deficit skills (Swicegood, 1994). Additionally, students who prepare portfolios gain management skills and acquire ownership in their portfolio by determining, with the instructor, what will be included.

Although definition, type, and quality of portfolio assessment vary, most researchers agree that the following items should be included: (a) a table of contents or sections detailing what is included in the portfolio, (b) an explanation of the included materials and why they were selected, (c) behavior and adaptive functioning data, (d) strategic learning and self-regulation data, and (e) academic or functional academic data. Furthermore, samples for the portfolio should be selected from a variety of settings and procedures, using both raw data and evaluation feedback. Finally, the portfolio should be housed in a container such as a binder, folder, or notebook (Hendrick-Keefe, 1995; Swicegood, 1994; Wesson & King, 1992).

Critics point to a lack of empirical evidence demonstrating that portfolio assessment is an effective evaluation tool, including lack of guidelines for its use, lack of information about the effects on teaching and learning, and lack of information about the impact on student motivation (Nolet, 1992). Although little research has been conducted on using portfolio assessment with students with Asperger Syndrome, the combination of quantitative and qualitative data it yields may offer a clearer picture of a student's functional abilities. In addition, portfolios may initiate positive instructor–student–family interactions, while providing students with valuable decision-making opportunities (Hendrick-Keefe, 1995; Swicegood, 1994).

Students with Asperger Syndrome can verbally participate in developing portfolio goals. They may help choose the materials and describe their experiences in the portfolio. These students may benefit from a videotaped interview included in their portfolio. For example, an instructor could ask the student questions about school tasks such as "Did you like the class?" "What made it easy or hard?" and " What would you like to do in this area in the future?"

Ecobehavioral Assessment

Ecobehavioral assessment provides information on a student's behavior through manipulation of the environment and other ecological factors (Kamps, Leonard, Dugan, Boland, & Greenwood, 1991). Thus, ecobehavioral assessment examines both the behavior and the ecological factors that support it. One ecobehavioral assessment technique is behavior acceleration (Greenwood, Carta, & Atwater, 1991). Behavior acceleration examines desired behaviors and the skills necessary for success in a specific situation. For example, a person's behavior is assessed within the demands of the classroom, work setting, and home. Instructional materials, as well as the student's attitude toward and interactions with the instructors are also examined. The resulting information allows for the development of interventions that will accelerate the behavior, improve the instruction, or both. Ecological assessment requires a great deal of examiner time but can yield useful information about instructional practices and setting demands that can significantly affect a student's success.

Translating Assessment Results into Meaningful Procedures

After conducting observations, scoring protocols, and analyzing test results, the examiner must synthesize the data to clarify the student's performance status. Synthesis is the interpretation and integration of findings or information. A synthesis of assessment results describes the meaning of test results or observations and provides insight into how this information can affect instructional strategies. The synthesis process may well be the most important aspect of any assessment battery. It is customary for a synthesis to be presented as a written report, along with other information such as anecdotal observations, test scores, and recommendations. Although the format of the synthesis is flexible, depending on the components of the assessment, certain groupings are helpful when organizing a report for a student with Asperger Syndrome: (a) cognitive and motor skills, (b) communication and language skills, (c) behavior and social/emotional development, and (d) problem-solving skills.

Three basic types of statements should be included in the assessment report: information, inferences, and judgments (Moran, 1995). Information is specific and verifiable. An information statement includes only facts about what occurred during testing and observation. Information should be stated as quantifiable outcomes or in concrete terms such as "hit," "kick," and "bite" rather than "aggressive behavior." An example of an information statement is "Andy hit the examiner's right hand three times while attempting the puzzle activity."

Inference statements are less specific than information statements and may include interpretive comments that go beyond the observable facts. Therefore, inferences are more subjective than information and cannot be directly verified. The majority of the synthesis in an assessment report consists of inference statements. For example, if David did not complete five out of six items on a particular subtest, the examiner could infer that David did not possess the necessary skills to perform at that skill level.

Judgment statements are usually contained in the final section of the assessment report. They are both general and subjective. Thus, judgment statements can be recommendations or diagnoses that combine inferences and information. For example, a judgment statement might be "Diane should receive reading instruction in a one-on-one setting specially designed for students with Asperger Syndrome."

Identifying Student Strengths and Concerns

An assessment report should include a specific and clear list of the student's areas of strength and concern. It is recommended that a two-column format be used for the list of strengths and concerns. In one column, the specific strength or concern is listed; in the other column, evidence is provided. For example, when the examiner writes "recognizes complex parts of a whole" in the concern column, he or she provides direct evidence for the concern, such as "did not complete interlocking puzzle," in the other column. This format allows readers to instantly recognize specific student strengths and target behaviors.

The detailing of the student's strengths is especially helpful in developing an educational plan that fosters the student's knowledge and skills. For example, if a student can recognize single-word directions such as "sit" or "drink" during testing, the examiner can make a recommendation such as "Provide Johnny opportunities to follow a variety of single-word directions, then gradually shift this pattern of commands to include two or more words."

Owning Assessment Results

The final step in the assessment process is the dissemination of results. The benefits of assessment should be shared by the students themselves, their parents, their teachers, and others involved in their educational life. The examiner should meet with the student, his or her parents, and relevant professionals to view and interpret assessment results.

Before the meeting, the examiner must prepare the assessment report. If the examiner determines that additional information might be helpful in developing interventions for the student, he or she attaches copies of articles or other documents as appendices. The examiner also plans an appropriate agenda for the meeting. When this preparation is finished, the examiner schedules the meeting.

At the meeting, the examiner should create a positive, interactive atmosphere. According to Moran (1995), all parties at the meeting should (a) have a mutual respect for each participant's competency, (b) realize that each person has a unique but equally valuable skill to offer, (c) regard all participants as equals, and (d) remain flexible about recommendations. Participants may have difficulty understanding specific terminology related to the assessment process and the different disciplines represented at the meeting. The examiner can avoid misinterpretations by promptly clarifying terminology and avoiding professional jargon as much as possible. Although the examiner will most likely assume a leadership role, presenting strengths, concerns, and recommendations based on the assessment data, it is important that all participants feel comfortable and welcome to make suggestions and discuss personal perspectives.

By meeting to discuss the assessment results, all participants can share information and gain direction for educational planning for the student with Asperger Syndrome. For professionals, the assessment interpretation can be a valuable tool for creating individualized interventions. For parents, the meeting may help remove anxiety about their child's disability and build an understanding of how professionals will work with the child. Moreover, the assessment interpretation provides professionals involved in the student's educational plan an excellent opportunity to share different perspectives. Finally, ownership of assessment results by all persons involved in the education of a student with Asperger Syndrome, including the student himself or herself, provides the atmosphere of a team working to assist the student in overcoming the challenges of Asperger Syndrome.

Developing Assessment-Based Intervention Strategies

When assessment allows for a thorough investigation of a student's strengths and concerns, it becomes a useful tool for developing educational intervention strategies. For students with Asperger Syndrome, assessment provides a direct link for establishing quality service, because many of these students do not function well in the classroom without individualized curricula. Students with Asperger Syndrome demonstrate a wide range of discrepancies in skills and capabilities. Many have limited generalization abilities and unique information processing functions. Teachers and other professionals are required to provide educational services that are precisely matched with the individual's needs. Therefore, integration of educational intervention and thorough, ongoing assessment enables individualized educational services for students with Asperger Syndrome.

It is not a simple task to establish a routine of assessment-based intervention in daily school life. Assessment-based intervention begins with an examination of the student's specific strengths and concerns as revealed by the evaluation. The professional draws on the strengths to establish short- and long-range objectives to address deficits. The professional uses feedback on preferred teaching styles and response modes to select and develop curriculum and instructional procedures. The process concludes where it began—with a continual reexamination of the individual's skills and abilities and modifications to the intervention procedures. Thus, the cycle of testing, teaching, and modifying continues throughout the student's educational life.

Basic Assumptions of Assessment

Assessment attempts to examine and evaluate complex human nature. Therefore, it is impossible to obtain perfect data. However, individuals involved in assessment should be aware of threats to the quality of their data collection and should attempt to avoid them to maximize the assessment's validity. Newland (1973) presented five basic assumptions underlying a valid assessment, which have held true over the years: (a) The person administering the test is skilled, (b) error will be present, (c) acculturation is comparable, (d) behavior sample is adequate, and (e) present behavior is observed and future behavior is inferred. Table 2.5 provides further detail on these basic assumptions.

Training for Assessment

Assessment of students with Asperger Syndrome should be conducted by qualified personnel who are familiar with the characteristics, response patterns, and idiosyncratic behaviors of this population. Unfortunately, few training programs currently specialize in the assessment of persons with Asperger Syndrome. However, it is possible to learn general assessment techniques through many university programs or

Table 2.5
Basic Assumptions of Assessment

The person administering the test is skilled.

Before administering any test to a student, an examiner must be appropriately trained. The examiner must know the content, characteristics, administration, scoring, and interpretation of the test. It is critical that an examiner does not conduct any assessment procedure for which he or she is not qualified.

Error will be present.

There is no perfect educational or psychological measurement. Differences in the testing environment, differences between examiners, changes in the student, or unexpected events during the testing always exist. Moreover, standardized and commercially produced tests are not error-free. As much as possible, examiners must attempt to control for errors in testing, and test interpretation should reflect the expected error levels.

Acculturation is comparable.

This assumption primarily pertains to norm-referenced or standardized tests. Norm-referenced tests compare a student's performance with that of a normative sample. The sample's performance on the test has been statistically averaged by age, grade level, or both. For an accurate score and an appropriate interpretation, the student being tested should approximately match the normative sample with respect to sex, race, ethnicity, and experiential background. Experiential background is critical, as it reflects how the student has developed as a result of his or her learning experiences. It is important to note that many commercially produced norm-referenced tests are developed using normative samples of students without disabilities.

Behavior sample is adequate.

In behavior samples, the quantity and the quality of the data must be considered. For behavioral assessment, examiners need to establish both what they observe and how they rate what they observe. For example, in observing how a male student with Asperger Syndrome initiates interactions with others, Examiner A might observe the student once and note that he could not initiate any social interactions during 30 minutes in a socially rich environment (e.g., recess, lunch). Examiner B might observe the student on five similar occasions for 20 minutes each time and note that the student initiated social interactions twice. Examiner C, after observing the student on three occasions during a peer tutoring session, might note that the student correctly maintained three social interactions. Clearly, all examiners viewed the same process; however, the data reported are quite varied. Examiner A did not observe the student with sufficient frequency, and Examiner C was rating a different behavior. The observation of different behaviors, use of different examination criteria, or both makes the data incomparable. Thus, the examiner must plan in advance how much data should be collected to yield valid results and what types of measurement would be appropriate to assess specific behaviors.

Present behavior is observed and future behavior is inferred.

During the assessment process, only the student's present performance can be observed. Examiners make inferences about the student's capabilities and future performance from this limited observational data.

---

through workshop and inservice training offered by local school districts or other educational institutions. Many basic assessment techniques are applicable to all types of students. Thus, after learning general assessment techniques, a practitioner can modify the procedures according to the needs of the type of student being assessed. Table 2.6 provides a framework for learning and practicing assessment of students with Asperger Syndrome.

Table 2.6
Training for Assessment

Knowledge of Asperger Syndrome

Before conducting any assessment, an examiner must have a general understanding of Asperger Syndrome. Without this knowledge, the examiner cannot appropriately modify general assessment techniques. For example, if an examiner knows how to administer an aptitude test but does not recognize a common speech pattern of Asperger Syndrome called perseveration, the examiner cannot adequately interpret the unusual verbal pattern observed during testing. Preferably, an examiner would have prior experience working with students with Asperger Syndrome before conducting any assessment.

Knowledge of assessment

Assessment requires thorough planning. However, this planning cannot be done without an ample knowledge of assessment. This reciprocal interaction is imperative for conducting appropriate testing. Knowledge of assessment includes understanding different kinds of data, observational techniques, formal and informal procedures, scoring, interpretation of data, and troubleshooting.

Basic knowledge of statistics

Advanced knowledge of statistics is not required for most assessments. However, because assessment covers many types of data, an examiner should, at minimum, understand the basics of statistics for an accurate interpretation of the data. For example, most norm-referenced tests use standard scores. Without an understanding of this concept, the examiner will find little or no meaning in the test scores. Fortunately, many educational assessment publications, as well as test administration manuals, include information on basic statistics.

Practice

As with teaching students with Asperger Syndrome, knowledge itself does not ensure good application. An ability to conduct meaningful assessment requires thorough practice and feedback. Therefore, it is recommended that the examiner assist with an assessment before attempting solo administration. Furthermore, having a mentor to monitor the examiner's performance during initial assessments can be invaluable. Practice not only helps develop assessment skills but also builds confidence in administration and interpretation.

Concluding Thoughts

Many different types of assessment procedures are available for students with Asperger Syndrome. Thus, professionals must select a battery of measures most appropriate for each individual student. Norm-referenced tests and developmental assessments are suitable for initial diagnosis, periodic comprehensive overview, and summative evaluation. Informal assessment techniques can be chosen for daily or ongoing formative evaluation of student skills. Finally, ecobehavioral measures allow for physical and interactive modifications to the learning environment. Together, these tools can yield a comprehensive picture of a student's abilities and needs, allowing practitioners and families to work collaboratively to create the optimal learning environment for a student with Asperger Syndrome.

CHAPTER

TEACHING ACADEMIC CONTENT TO STUDENTS WITH ASPERGER SYNDROME

School is a complex environment that requires students to use cognitive, social, behavioral, and motor skills to prosper and grow. Students with Asperger Syndrome have many strengths, particularly in the cognitive domain, that can contribute to school success; however, when cognitive demands are paired with other environmental demands (e.g., social demands, lack of structure), these students' achievement may not parallel their potential. Students with Asperger Syndrome also have very specific talents; they tend to excel when they are given concrete, visual stimuli but experience problems when abstractions are used. The social nature of the school environment also requires consideration. Students with Asperger Syndrome generally want to interact with others but often do not understand the rules of social relationships. Thus, the environment makes a variety of structural, academic, and social demands, many of which are not well defined. Students with Asperger Syndrome have difficulty coping with each of these demands individually; when they are combined, school can become a confusing, frustrating, and sometimes frightening place.

Characteristics That Affect Academic Performance

Students with Asperger Syndrome are typically of average or above-average intelligence. In fact, intelligence quotients (IQ) in persons with Asperger Syndrome have been documented in the gifted range. Because of their IQ level, students with Asperger Syndrome are often expected to perform at the same level as their peers. Although some students can meet this expectation, many cannot. However, it is often difficult for teachers to detect that students may not be completing their work in a meaningful way. As mentioned in Chapter 2, these students are able to mask their inability to understand and perform certain tasks. Because their disabilities are usually counteracted by their abilities, students with Asperger Syndrome give the impression that they are competent in many skill areas in which they actually have deficits.

It is difficult to identify the specific areas of ability and disability of persons with Asperger Syndrome because of their heterogeneity. A person with Asperger Syndrome may exhibit problems in two, three, four, or even more areas of functioning. Further, these deficits may be moderate to severe.

The goal of this chapter is to give an overview of some areas of academic functioning that may be impaired in persons with Asperger Syndrome. The appearance of each impairment and its severity vary among individuals. Instructional strategies that can enhance academic success are also described.

Distraction/Inattention

Persons with Asperger Syndrome often receive a diagnosis of Attention-Deficit/Hyperactivity Disorder (ADHD) at one time in their lives. The conditions have many commonalities, particularly related to distractibility and inattentiveness. Attention often seems fleeting. One moment, the student with Asperger Syndrome may appear to be attending, then he or she suddenly seems to withdraw into an inner world and be totally unaware of the environment. Teacher directions are not processed; student conversations are not heard. This daydreaming may occur over extended periods, with no predictability. The daydreaming is often so intense that a physical prompt from the teacher is needed to call the student back to task. Often the antecedent is unknown.

Even while attending, the student may not react to teacher instructions. For example, the student may start to follow a three-step direction but appear to lose focus as he or she completes the first phase. Rather than looking for a model or asking for help, the student looks for a way out. The student may remain frozen in that place, wander aimlessly about, shuffle through the desk, stare into space, or begin to daydream. On rare occasions, the student may cause a distraction or act out. Often these same behaviors are seen when the student is required to engage in nonpreferred work tasks for extended periods.

Social interactions are often distracting for students with Asperger Syndrome. Because these students want to interact with others in general, they often focus all of their attention on others in the classroom instead of on the tasks at hand. If the student with Asperger Syndrome has a particularly strong need to interact with a specific classmate, he or she may attend to that person exclusively, staring nonstop at the person or listening to that person's conversations. If the student with Asperger Syndrome and the classmate have developed a reciprocal relationship, the student with Asperger Syndrome might unilaterally seek that person's approval before beginning a task or addressing the teacher or another student. This gives the peer an enormous amount of power over the person with Asperger Syndrome, which can be used in a negative way. For example, the peer may prompt the student with Asperger Syndrome to complete assignments for him or her, ask the student to break classroom rules, or prompt the student to engage in activities that will place him or her in harm's way.

Students with Asperger Syndrome are often distracted because they do not know how to discern relevant from irrelevant stimuli. A student with Asperger Syndrome might focus on a particular picture or map in a textbook while other students in the class have moved on to the next chapter. This student might focus on the way a speaker's earring dangles when she moves her head instead of listening to the content of her lecture. The student with Asperger Syndrome may become highly frustrated when he or she attempts to memorize every fact associated with Columbus's discovering America as mentioned in the text, including an extensive list of food and supplies carried on each ship. The student does not innately know that memorizing such information is not necessary.

Tunnel Vision

School requires that students attend to certain stimuli while screening out irrelevant, yet competing distractors. That is, at any given time a student might be expected to attend to a textbook and ignore (a) students talking around her, (b) a teacher offering another student help, and (c) a bulletin board about a favored topic. This is often difficult for the student with Asperger Syndrome for several reasons.

On one level, the student with Asperger Syndrome often cannot discern what others deem relevant. If the bulletin board contains information on a topic of high interest, the student may consider it more important than a text. If a student with Asperger Syndrome has a strong social attachment to someone across the room, interacting with that person might take precedence over any task the teacher assigns. Rational explanations that talking across the room is inappropriate may not affect the student with Asperger Syndrome. This student might seem "driven" to interact with his friend.

Tunnel vision also operates in a second way. Students with Asperger Syndrome logically group items or characteristics so that they make sense to them. That is, they form a schema that is exact and often inflexible. For example, a student who learns the spelling rule "i before e except after c" might apply the rule rigidly. The student would be convinced that words like *neighbor* and *weigh* should be spelled *nieghbor* and *wiegh*.

Problems can present themselves when the student is reading for information. Generally, reading for information is a difficult task. Students with Asperger Syndrome will most likely read to find specific information presented in a text study guide while ignoring and simply not processing in a meaningful way information that they were not responsible for. When the student is later tested on the text and given questions that were not in the study guide, he or she will most likely not answer those questions or answer them incorrectly, even if the information seems obvious to others.

Student obsessions are another hallmark of tunnel vision. Two types of obsessions are typically exhibited by students with Asperger Syndrome. The first type of obsession (primary) is one where the student has an all-encompassing level of interest in a particular topic. As a result, a discussion of this topic can escalate to almost tantrum-like behavior, where the student cannot control his or her discussion of the topic and behavior. Rapid speech, increased volume, a high-pitched voice, pacing, and hand wringing often occur with primary obsessions. Primary obsessions typically do not lend themselves to rational discussions and explorations. Indeed, students who have this type of obsession seem to discuss the topic in an almost circular fashion.

Secondary obsessions, on the other hand, are marked interests about which the student remains lucid, focused, and ready to learn about the particular topic. Students actively seek new information about the topic, but can be somewhat easily redirected. Secondary interests are often used by teachers to motivate students to complete academic tasks. In some cases, secondary obsessions develop into career interests.

Some professionals who work with students with Asperger Syndrome speculate that distraction/inattention and tunnel vision are prominent features of this disability—that these factors are the overriding characteristics that affect and influence the other deficit areas. Although these professionals acknowledge that rote memory may be a problem, they maintain that it is in large part due to the distraction/inattention and tunnel vision that occur when students attempt to use their rote memory skills.

Rote Memory

Rote memory skills are generally well developed in persons with Asperger Syndrome. Case studies document that some children have learned to recite words they see in written format by age 3. Others have reported that young children with Asperger Syndrome have been able to repeat paragraphs of information after seeing them only once. However, the comprehension level of many of these persons does not appear to match their rote skills. Comprehension is often at the factual level. That is, persons with Asperger Syndrome can understand basic facts in written material and either repeat them verbatim or paraphrase them. Many, however, experience difficulty understanding vocabulary in context and reading for information. Thus, persons with Asperger Syndrome may give the false impression that they understand concepts because they are able to parrot responses. As a result, it is easy for a teacher to mistake rote responses for content mastery and urge the student to master more difficult material. Students may be able to repeat algebra equations but be unable to perform them. Similarly, they may be able to answer multiple-choice questions about a novel they have read but be unable to analyze character intent in a cooperative group setting.

Rote memory may be nonproductive for students with Asperger Syndrome in another way. Educators assume that a good rote memory means that students can remember, at any time, pieces of information or events. But this is not true for many persons with Asperger Syndrome. Although they can store chunks of information in memory, they often have difficulty determining how to retrieve the information. Open-ended questions such as "Tell me what the main character in the story did after his horse disappeared" may not trigger a response because the student has stored the information under the main character's name and is unable to make the transition from the term "main character" to the character's name. In students with Asperger Syndrome, therefore, an exceptional memory is not related to the ability to recall information.

A third way in which rote memory may be nonproductive in persons with Asperger Syndrome is related to integration of learned material and experience. These students may memorize entire inventories of facts or directions, but these lists often remain unconnected bits of information. For example, a student with Asperger Syndrome could memorize the list of supplies to bring to each of his six middle-school classes and recite them when the appropriate trigger or key word was supplied. But this same student might forget to bring a pencil to class. Another student might remember to bring a pencil to class, but arrive with it unsharpened. She knows from past experience that the pencil must have a point to be a useful tool but somehow does not connect this bit of information to her present need. Although by adolescence these students have memorized innumerable bits of academic information, their knowledge tends to be fragmented and of limited utility.

Visual Versus Auditory Processing

Many students with Asperger Syndrome learn and process information in a manner that is generally incompatible with the way academic information is presented. Whereas most academic information is presented orally, students with Asperger Syndrome often have difficulty with auditory input. Processing difficulties may occur for one of three reasons.

First, the student can understand and follow directions in sentences and indeed understands sentences, if additional processing time is given. However, because the words are presented orally, the student has nothing on which to reflect.

Second, the student may understand individual words used by a teacher or student, but may not understand what the words mean when they are used in the context of sentences and paragraphs. The student requires additional processing time to understand the meaning of the words as they are used in sentences. If the student attempts to memorize the words using rote memory skills, it is almost as if there is little cognitive energy left with which to process meaning.

Third, it is speculated that students with Asperger Syndrome possess at least average ability to process visual as well as auditory information. However, when asked to process both types of information concurrently, they are often unable to do so.

Information must be presented in one modality or the other to facilitate processing; otherwise, overload occurs.

Structure

Students with Asperger Syndrome typically fall at the ends of the structure continuum: They either have an inherent ability to provide structure or totally rely on others to help them organize themselves. It is often said that students with Asperger Syndrome have either the neatest or messiest desks in class.

Generally, it is easier for persons with Asperger Syndrome to function in an organized environment. Predictable schedules, uniform assignment formats, and consistent teacher affect help these students devote their time and energy to academic tasks. Those who have internal structure often have rigid expectations that schedules be followed and commitments be honored; unscheduled events cause these students great discomfort that can be manifested as disorientation, refusal to engage in the new activity, extended discourse about the canceled or postponed event, or behavior problems. In other words, the student communicates through language and behavior that change is difficult.

Educators comment that they have seen a student with Asperger Syndrome tolerate change in some instances but lose control when the environment was altered. Sometimes students with Asperger Syndrome can tolerate change, if that change occurs in only one dimension. For example, if library time is changed the student may adjust to the new schedule. However, if library time and the librarian are changed simultaneously, the same student may have difficulty maintaining any type of self-control.

Most students with Asperger Syndrome have a limited ability to structure their own environment. A messy person with Asperger Syndrome probably has not made a conscious choice to be that way; rather, he or she lacks good organizational skills. A student with this disability can literally lose a paper received only 1 minute earlier. He never has a pencil in class. The note that the teacher placed in the student's backpack never makes it home. Written work is not placed uniformly on a page. A middle-school student's locker is a mess; she often cannot locate her locker combination and when she does, she cannot find what she needs inside. She cannot organize her day by bringing her science and math books to science class, even though math class follows immediately in the room next door. Almost every facet of the student's life is in disarray. Teachers and parents often wonder how the student with Asperger Syndrome gets from one place to another. It is a challenge to organize this type of student. Merely providing a schedule or list of supplies is not enough. These aids are most often lost.

Problem Solving

Although students are often able to engage in high-level thinking and problem solving when their area of interest is involved, these skills are often not generalized throughout the school day. Many students with Asperger Syndrome select one problem-solving strategy and use it consistently regardless of the situation. Persistence is common in persons with Asperger Syndrome. For example, if the school locker does not open, the student may keep trying the combination. Although this strategy can be effective, there needs to be a self-monitoring component. If the student has tried the combination five times unsuccessfully, chances are that there is another problem with the locker. Persistence, if unsuccessful, can result in a behavioral outburst because the student with Asperger Syndrome might not know the problem-solving strategy of asking an adult or peer when difficulty arises.

Other students with Asperger Syndrome may have learned several problem-solving strategies, but may not have generalized their use. For example, the student with Asperger Syndrome may know to use a dictionary to find a word meaning in English class, but not realize that the same technique may also be effective in understanding a term in science.

There is also the problem of recall related to problem solving. Although a student may know a host of problem-solving strategies and realize that they can be generalized, she may not be able to recall any strategies when they are needed. Because the student with Asperger Syndrome often has difficulty searching his or her memory for particular facts, the student may not be able to access the strategy. Even if a student has an effective system for retrieving problem-solving strategies, it is still likely that he cannot use this system. By the time the student cognitively realizes that a problem exists, he is typically so confused, angry, or disoriented that his reaction is behavioral—a tantrum or withdrawal.

Problem solving becomes even more difficult in academics if abstract concepts are involved. Thus, students with Asperger Syndrome frequently have difficulty with word problems, estimation, algebra, and geometry—all of which require problem-solving skills and often contain a high level of abstraction.

Problem-solving difficulties are also apparent outside the field of mathematics. Teachers often give assignments that require students to take the role of a historical character. Students often write papers or plays or make speeches as a historical figure. Tasks of this nature are difficult for those who do not understand the human experience from different perspectives. Persons with Asperger Syndrome have difficulty understanding their own state of mind; therefore, they cannot be expected to imagine the state of mind of others.

Motor Skills

Motor problems that are often seen in persons with Asperger Syndrome affect academic performance. Specifically, students with Asperger Syndrome are typically clumsy, have an unusual gait, have difficulty with pencil grasp, and write illegibly. Gross-motor problems may lead to fear of heights and the inability to jump over obstacles, skip, or catch or throw a ball. Fine-motor difficulties mean that students may not be motivated to complete work because of the enormous amount of energy required to write. Students who consent to write often turn in assignments that are unreadable. As a result, they are often told to rewrite the page and try to be neater. Requests like this result in negative reactions. Depending on the student's behavioral repertoire, reactions may include refusal to do the task, withdrawal, ignoring the teacher, daydreaming, or an overt display directed toward self, peers, or the teacher.

Motivation

Students with Asperger Syndrome are often not motivated to complete a task just because it was assigned by the teacher. If the task does not make sense in the scheme of the student's life, chances are he or she will see no reason to invest time and energy. "When will I use algebra, anyway?" is a frequent question. Teacher statements such as "You need to do it because I said so" often do not have the desired impact on the student with Asperger Syndrome. Even if the task has relevance to everyday life, the student may not make that connection.

Engaging a student in extensive rhetoric to convince him of the importance of the assignment may not be effective for several reasons. Even if the student is apt to listen to the teacher's explanation, he may not understand the abstract concepts used by the teacher to link the assignment with "real-life" needs. Another student with Asperger Syndrome may like the teacher rhetoric because the focus is removed from the task at hand, and the student does not have to complete the assignment, at least in the short run.

Obsessions, particularly secondary obsessions, often serve as effective motivators for students with Asperger Syndrome. Once a topic of interest is identified, the student appears to spend the majority of time reflecting and acting on it in a somewhat rational and lucid manner. As a result, the student with Asperger Syndrome is typically highly motivated to learn more about the area of obsession and is anxious to share knowledge with others. This information sharing occurs regardless of the interest level of the listeners.

Individuals with Asperger Syndrome are often motivated by people they like; conversely, they may refuse to engage in activities or complete tasks if they involve people with whom they would rather not interact. Thus, it is important that students with Asperger Syndrome be assigned to teachers who have the potential to develop positive, reciprocal relationships with them.

Motivation is also linked to the student's mistaken impression that he or she has control over a variety of situations. When the teacher announces that everyone did poorly on the spelling test, it is not uncommon for a student with Asperger Syndrome to think that she is to blame. Egocentricity dictates that the person with Asperger Syndrome is at the center of most events and directly affects the performance of others. There may be a profound sense of burden because the student feels at fault.

Effective Instructional Strategies

Students with Asperger Syndrome have endless potential when teachers recognize their individual needs and characteristics and structure the environment for success. The use of visual and structural strategies, as well as an appropriate instructional sequence, can help the student attend to and profit from instruction. Being in a motivational environment, understanding the hidden curriculum, and having a teacher whose style matches the student's needs can also enhance school success.

Visual Strategies

As previously mentioned, students with Asperger Syndrome benefit when information is presented visually rather than auditorily. Visual information is more concrete than auditory information and allows for greater processing time.

Visual Schedules

Visual schedules take an abstract concept such as time and present it in a more concrete and manageable form. They can yield multiple benefits for children and youth with Asperger Syndrome, who often exhibit visual strengths. For example, visual schedules allow students to anticipate upcoming events and activities, develop an understanding of time, and predict change. Further, they can be used to stimulate communication through the discussion of past, present, and future events, increase on-task behavior, facilitate transition between activities, and teach new skills.

Visual schedules are based on the strengths and needs of the student. Using student characteristics, a visual schedule may be based on levels of visual representation. As would be expected, the more abstract the visual schedule, the higher the level of representation. Table 3.1 represents the hierarchy of visual representation from highest to lowest level of abstraction.

Table 3.1
Level of Abstraction for Visual Schedules

Level of abstraction	Visual representation
highest ↑↓ lowest	written phrase or sentence written word black-and-white line drawing colored drawing photograph miniature object full-sized object

For young students who require concrete visual cues to understand upcoming events, the teacher can design an object schedule that uses the actual materials from each of the scheduled activities. For example, if a math lesson requires the use of colored blocks as manipulatives, then the colored blocks may be used to represent math.

Older, more advanced students may benefit from schedules that use colored drawings of the student completing the activity, drawings, written words, or sentences. It is important to determine which level of visual representation is appropriate for each student and then pair it with the next higher level. For example, if a student is functioning at the photograph level, a colored drawing can be paired with the photograph to introduce the higher-level concept. Similarly, if a student is functioning at the black-and-white drawing level, written words can be paired with the drawing.

Schedule arrangement and placement options vary by student need and level of functioning. Schedules can be arranged left to right or top to bottom. Although either arrangement is acceptable, the left-to-right arrangement facilitates behavior required for reading. Schedules can take a variety of forms, which may include the following:

- placing the schedule in a photo album or three-ring binder
- hanging the schedule on the classroom wall with Velcro or masking tape
- placing the schedule in a pocket chart
- writing the schedule on a wipe-off board
- writing the schedule on a chalkboard
- typing the schedule on a piece of paper and placing it on the student's desk
- typing the schedule on an index card that will fit in the student's pocket or wallet
- writing the schedule on hole-punched cards that can hang on the student's belt loop with an O-ring

Students may enjoy and sometimes feel more comfortable when participating in the preparation of their schedule. This participation should occur first thing in the morning. Students can assist in assembling their schedule, copying it, or adding their own personal touch. This interactive time can also be used to review the daily routine, discuss changes, and reinforce rules.

Figures 3.1a and b and 3.2 provide samples of visual schedules. The first schedule was designed for a younger student with Asperger Syndrome who requires a moderate level of abstraction to understand the day's events. The second schedule is appropriate for students who have a high level of abstraction but require time and activity cues.

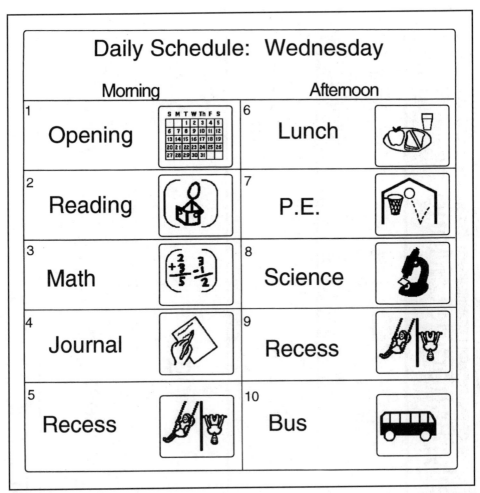

Figure 3.1a. Sample visual schedules for a student who functions at a moderate level of abstraction. Schedules made with the Boardmaker and Picture Communication Symbols. Picture Communication Symbols © 1987–1997 used with permission from the Mayer-Johnson Company, P.O. Box 1579, Solana Beach, CA 92075, 619-550-0084, fax 619-550-0449 (Mayerj@aol.com).

Daily Schedule: Monday

8:30	Calendar Time	
9:30	Seatwork	
10:30	Reading	
11:15	Recess	

Figure 3.1b. Continued.

8:00 a.m.	bus routine (put up coat and backpack, bathroom, review schedule with teacher or paraeducator)	
8:15 a.m.	breakfast	
8:30 a.m.	morning group	
9:00 a.m.	math activities	
10:00 a.m.	reading activities	
11:00 a.m.	adaptive physical education	
11:30 a.m.	lunch time	
12:00 p.m.	recess	
12:30 p.m.	work time (prevocational activity)	
1:30 p.m.	leisure time	
2:00 p.m.	language group	
2:30 p.m.	recess	
3:00 p.m.	music time	
3:15 p.m.	closing group	

Figure 3.2. Sample visual schedule for a student who functions at a high level of abstraction

Graphic Organizers

Graphic organizers provide a visual, holistic representation of facts and concepts within an organized framework. Graphic organizers arrange key terms to show their relationship to one another, providing abstract or implicit information in a concrete manner. They are particularly useful with content area material. Graphic organizers can be used before, during, or after students read a selection, either as an advance organizer or as a measure of concept attainment. Graphic organizers often enhance the learning of students with Asperger Syndrome because

- the visual modality is often a strength for these students;

- they remain consistent and constant, so that when the student "tunes in," they are available for viewing;

- they allow for processing time so the student can reflect on the written material at his or her own pace; and

- abstract information is presented in a concrete manner that is often more easily understood than a verbal presentation alone.

One type of graphic organizer is the semantic map. The focal point of the semantic map is the key word or concept enclosed in a geometric figure (e.g., circle or square) or in a pictorial representation of the word or concept. Lines or arrows connect this central shape to other shapes. Words or information related to the central concept are written on the connecting lines or in the other shapes. As the map expands, the words become more specific and detailed. For students who are young or who require additional cues, semantic maps can use pictures for the key words or concepts. Figures 3.3 and 3.4 provide examples of semantic maps.

Analogy graphic organizers are another strategy for students with Asperger Syndrome. The teacher selects two concepts for which the students will begin to identify attributes. The teacher and students define how the two concepts are alike and how they differ, then draw a conclusion. Often the teacher has to assist students in identifying attributes by presenting choices, either written or pictorial, from which the students select. This task can be completed individually, in small groups, or as a class. Figures 3.5 and 3.6 provide examples of two commonly used analogy graphic organizers: the Venn diagram and the compare/constrast chart.

Outlines

Because of motor and distraction/inattention problems, the student with Asperger Syndrome is often not good at taking notes on teacher lectures. Thus, teachers should help these students with note taking. The first step is to teach note taking. The student with Asperger Syndrome, as well as many other students, may neither understand the concept of main idea nor understand that teacher language cues students to salient

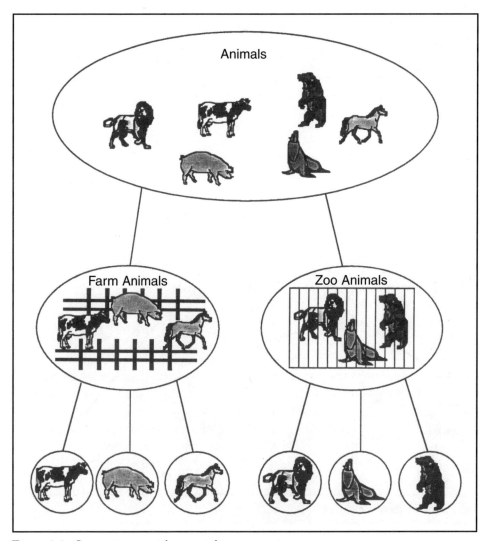

Figure 3.3. Semantic map with pictorial representation

information (i.e., when the teacher repeats an item or changes voice tone, the information is important). The teacher can assist the student by providing the following:

- A *complete outline*. This outline lists main points and details. It allows students to follow the lecture, but frees them from note taking.

- A *skeletal outline*. This outline lists main points. Students may use this format to fill in pertinent details delivered through lecture.

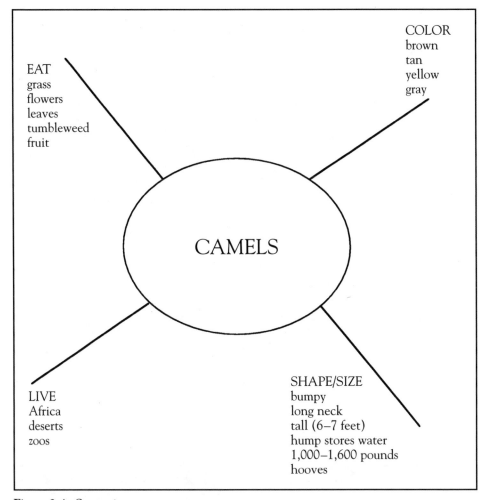

Figure 3.4. Semantic map

- *Direct verbal cues.* Verbal cues, such as "This is the first main point" or "This detail should be included in your notes," assist students in knowing which points to include in their notes. At this stage, students may be responsible for taking complete notes. The verbal cues serve as prompts.

- *Subtle verbal cues.* Subtle verbal cues also provide clues regarding important information. Students need to recognize these cues, such as "The *first* branch of the federal government is the legislative branch. Did you write that in your notes?" or "*You need to remember* that the legislative branch makes the laws."

The note-taking level of students with Asperger Syndrome must be considered when selecting the appropriate type of assistance. The types of assistance listed above

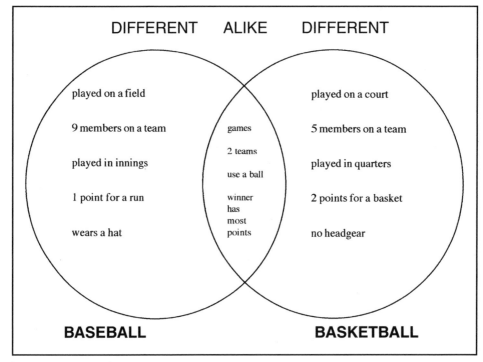

Figure 3.5. Venn diagram

can be considered hierarchical. When the student has mastered note taking at one level of assistance, the teacher can proceed to the next. Although they are hierarchical, types of assistance can be combined to facilitate the student's note taking. For example, a student with Asperger Syndrome may be able to work with a skeletal outline but require verbal cues to ensure that he notes the important details. It is important to note, however, that all students will not proceed up this hierarchy. Some students may always require a complete or skeletal outline.

Other note-taking options include having a peer take notes using carbon paper, with the copy going to the student with Asperger Syndrome, or allowing the student who is adept with the computer to take notes using outlining software.

Structural Strategies

Transitions, change, and organization are all problem areas for students with Asperger Syndrome. Teachers and parents must teach students the skills to meet these demands. For some students, instructional strategies are ineffective, and the environment must be adjusted to match their unique needs.

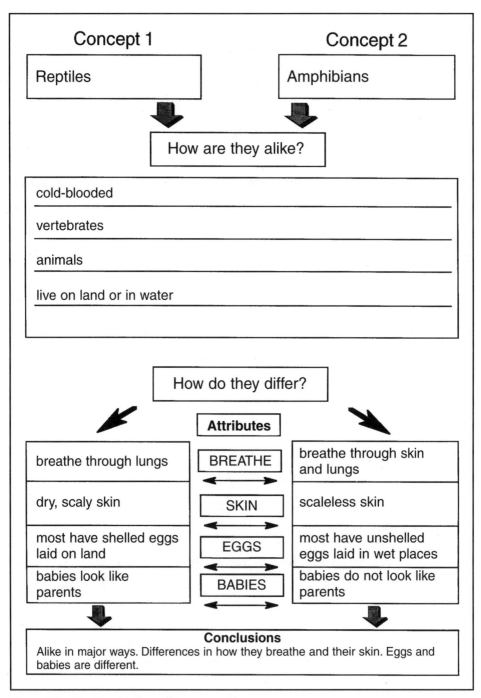

Figure 3.6. Compare/contrast chart

Preparation for Change

Students with Asperger Syndrome are typically routine-bound, and any schedule change can have deleterious effects on behavior. Thus, any major change in these students' schedules must be considered carefully. These students may need advance warning for fire drills, assemblies, pep rallies, or substitute teachers. Some students are so focused on routine that minor changes cause behavioral problems. For example, the seriously routine-bound student may not be able to adapt easily to a change in the daily reading lesson. This student, who is accustomed to doing a vocabulary exercise, oral reading, silent reading, and comprehension check, may lose control when the teacher varies the order of the activities or spends reading time playing a game of "Jeopardy" to test students' recall of the reading material.

Visual schedules that clearly outline what the student will be doing and what the expectations are for the new activity can help prepare these students for change. The teacher can write a one-time behavioral contract indicating the change, the tasks the student is responsible for completing, who will monitor the student, how the student will be monitored, and the reinforcement. The student and teacher review the document; after the teacher is certain that the student understands, both sign the document. The student can take the contract to the new situation and refer to it as necessary.

Buddy Program

A normally achieving peer who likes and understands the student with Asperger Syndrome can be an asset. Indeed, many parents have reported that a buddy or mentor has often made the difference in whether their children could cope with a school situation. Buddies can accompany these students during transitions, provide cues for appropriate behavior, and take notes for the students during class. In addition, buddies can provide the social interactions that many students with Asperger Syndrome desire but rarely succeed at unassisted.

Buddies must be carefully selected. They should be volunteers who understand the exceptionality, respect individual differences, and genuinely like the student. Typically, buddies should also be "model" students who are generally not susceptible to behaviors that parents and teachers would see as problematic (e.g., skipping school, acting disrespectfully toward adults and other students). Because students with Asperger Syndrome typically have poor social judgment, they might follow a peer into inappropriate social situations to have social interactions.

Early Release

Transitions between classes or to special activities (e.g., music, physical education) are often extremely disruptive to students with Asperger Syndrome. Unanticipated schedule changes often cause these students to experience a high stress level, and when this is combined with unfavorable environmental conditions (e.g., students bumping into each other, the student feeling that he or she needs to rush, a feeling of uncertainty about where the activity is located, taunting by peers), the student is likely to "fall apart." The student may have a tantrum, cry, "tune out," or refuse to comply. These behavioral problems often occur as a sort of self-protection. When the student is in a situation that he or she does not know how to handle, the student selects one of limited coping strategies, which is typically considered inappropriate by adults and peers.

These problems can be circumvented by providing the student with extra time to reach a destination. Releasing the student 5 minutes before the bell rings often provides a relatively stress-free environment (e.g., a hallway without many students, less noise) in which to get to a class, assembly, or other special event. This strategy may be particularly effective when combined with a transition buddy.

Assignment Notebooks

An effective organizational strategy for students with Asperger Syndrome is an assignment notebook, if homework is given. All homework tasks and their due dates are listed in the notebook. Ideally, the assignment notebook also contains a sample of what the assignment should look like. The teacher monitors the assignment notebook to ensure that all assignments and all supporting materials (e.g., samples, texts, worksheets) are included. Parents work cooperatively with the teacher by reviewing the notebook nightly and signing it as the student completes tasks.

Timelines

Teachers often assign tasks, such as book reports and term papers, that must be completed over an extended period of time. Typically, teachers will announce the task, explain the steps necessary to complete the assignment, and set a due date. The expectation is that students will budget their time to complete the assignment by the due date. Most students work on the assignment piece by piece over days or weeks. However, because of a variety of difficulties (e.g., lack of ability to structure tasks over time, inability to project how long a task will take, general disorganization, failure to understand the complexity of the task), students with Asperger Syndrome will often try to write a 20-page term paper or read a 200-page book and write a report in 2 hours the evening before the assignment is due.

Thus, teachers need to assist these students in budgeting their time. Teachers should create a list of steps needed to complete the task, help the student set target dates for completing each item, and establish a system to monitor the student over the course of the assignment. Monitoring should include asking to see the project at each stage, as the student with Asperger Syndrome may indicate that a task is completed when in fact it is not. This untruth may not be deliberate; it may be a function of the disability. For example, if a teacher says to a student, "I hope you understand that you should have your book read by now," the student may respond affirmatively, indicating an understanding of the statement but not connecting the statement to any action that she should have taken. It is best for teachers to enlist the aid of parents in developing and monitoring timelines; however, the teacher should not trust the student to be the sole source of communication between home and school.

Home Base

Students with Asperger Syndrome often view school as a stressful environment that presents several ongoing stressors of great magnitude, including difficulty predicting events because of changing schedules, tuning into and understanding teacher directions, and interacting with peers. Students with this exceptionality rarely indicate in any meaningful way that they are under stress or experiencing difficulty coping. Quite often they just tune out, daydream, or state in a monotone voice a seemingly benign phrase such as "I don't know what to do." Because no emotion is conveyed, these behaviors often go unnoticed by teachers. Then at some point a student acts verbally or physically aggressive, seemingly without provocation. The student may scream or kick over a desk. This behavior seems to be unpredictable.

Other students with Asperger Syndrome do not display these types of behaviors in school. Sometimes teachers report that these students do fine in school, even with academic and social problems. However, parents report that when these children arrive home, they lose control. They have a tantrum, cry, or are aggressive. It seems as if these students use all their self-control to manage at school, and once they get to a safe environment, they let go of some of the pressure they have bottled up inside.

What can educators do to help these students manage their stress at school and at home? In addition to instructing students on how to recognize and manage their stress levels, teachers can create a safe "home base" for students with Asperger Syndrome. This is a place where students can go when they feel the need to regain control. Resource rooms or counselors' offices can be safe places. When a student feels the need to leave the classroom, she can take assignments to the home base and work there in a less stressful environment. School personnel frequently schedule students' days so that they begin at the home base and then have frequent stops there. This allows students a teacher with whom they have a consistent relationship and a place to go when the need arises.

Instructional Sequence

Teachers must provide an instructional sequence that facilitates students' acquisition of information. This sequence includes effective lesson presentation and appropriate homework, if the teacher decides to assign it.

Rationale

Students with Asperger Syndrome often need to understand how or why concepts required for mastery are relevant. Thus, teachers must tell the student (a) why the information is useful, (b) how the student can use it, and (c) where it fits in with the knowledge the student already possesses. Similar to students with other exceptionalities, students with Asperger Syndrome need to understand lesson rationale before they can or will learn.

Direction

The teacher explains the goals for the content being presented and spells out exactly what the student needs to learn. Then using a direct instructional format, the instructor teaches the content using visual and auditory stimuli. The teacher breaks down the information and presents it in small increments. This type of instruction is active, with the teacher presenting information, asking questions, and providing corrective feedback. In other words, direct instruction is *not* presenting a worksheet with a model and telling the student to follow the directions.

Modeling

During the modeling phase, the teacher gets the student's attention and shows the student what he or she is supposed to do. The instructor demonstrates how to complete a worksheet, participate in a cooperative group activity, begin a project, and so forth. It is important for the teacher to demonstrate how to complete a task or assignment correctly, instead of telling the student what not to do. Many students with Asperger Syndrome know what they shouldn't do but have no understanding of what is required of them.

Models should be presented frequently. For some students with Asperger Syndrome, it may be necessary to present a model of how to put identifying information on a spelling test prior to each examination. The teacher should spell out every direction for these students, preferably with a visual component. The teacher cannot assume that a student knows to number his spelling paper to 20 just because he has always had 20 spelling words. Anything that is only implied by the teacher will likely not be understood by these students.

Interpretation

Throughout the lesson, the teacher must closely monitor the student's emotional state. Because students with Asperger Syndrome often have a flat, even seemingly negative affect, it is difficult to tell when they are stressed as a result of not comprehending specific content. The teacher must work with the student to understand how he or she communicates emotional distress and meet that student's needs through additional instruction, modeling, or individual work sessions. Failure to engage in this very important step can result in the student's tuning out or having a behavioral outburst.

Verification

Because of a propensity for tunnel vision and distraction/inattention, the student with Asperger Syndrome must be actively engaged throughout the instructional process.

The student should be provided physical cues to attend to relevant stimuli and be asked frequent questions. Physical cues could come in the form of the teacher staying close by and tapping briefly on the student's desk or using a prearranged signal (clearing the throat, placing a pencil on the student's desk, placing a hand on the student's shoulder). For the student with Asperger Syndrome who requires a long processing time, the teacher might want to arrange a strategy so that the student knows when he or she will be asked a question. For example, the teacher might tell a student that she will be asked a question only when the teacher stands next to her. The teacher can then use this strategy, initially asking the student questions to which he or she knows the answers. No one else in the class needs to be aware that the student and teacher have this agreement.

A second strategy involves telling the student in advance what questions he or she will be asked during class. The questions could be presented in written format, oral format, or both depending on the student's needs. The student will then be able to relax, process, and learn from the lecture without worrying about being unprepared to answer questions.

Homework

Teachers and parents or caregivers should work together to determine whether homework should be assigned and if so, how much. Because students with Asperger Syndrome have a marked need for structure, it is often best to assign tasks that can be completed at the home base or during a study hall.

If homework is assigned, it is best to use an assignment notebook and a parent-teacher communication system. This structure is necessary because parents or caregivers will play an active role in ensuring that the student completes assignments. Parents or caregivers need to set up a structure for assignment completion and monitoring similar to what the teachers use in school. In addition, they will most likely need to assist the student by clarifying and giving an overview of assignments. In some cases, a parent may need to model the task for the student. Thus, teachers should ensure that the parents or caregivers understand the homework. This is often difficult, because the teacher cannot simply send home a note to the parents—chances are it will never reach its destination. The disorganized student with Asperger Syndrome will misplace the note or bury it in the bottom of the backpack and forget that it is there. To facilitate home–school communcation, some schools have established a homework line that students and parents can call to hear an overview of assigned work. This sort of system is ideal for the student with Asperger Syndrome and his or her caregivers.

Motivation

Many students with Asperger Syndrome are difficult to motivate. They often see no reason to complete a task and frequently verbalize this to the teacher in a less than tactful, even blunt, manner (e.g., "This makes no sense," "No one in the world does anything like this," "This is stupid."). These students are not intentionally being rude, but merely stating what they consider to be a fact.

There are some general ways to motivate the student with Asperger Syndrome.

- A rationale will often motivate the student to begin an assignment. However, if the student is one who likes to engage in verbal power struggles, giving a reason for completing an assignment may start a series of "Yes, but . . ." statements or reasons why the rationale is not relevant to the student.

- Another way to prompt the student to complete a task is to acknowledge the student's statement and then provide a global rule (e.g., "I know you think that no one does work like this, but everyone in the class needs to do at least three of these problems. Please start here.").

- Assignments that relate to student obsessions are often highly motivating, if the obsession is a secondary one. In their desire to discuss, learn, and read about their particular interest, these students will often eagerly complete an assignment on the topic.

- A fourth way to motivate is to use the Premack Principle, or "Grandma's Rule." The teacher can set a contingency on a visual schedule that says following completion of a nonpreferred task, the student can engage in a preferred activity.

- Often it is motivating for the student to complete an assignment with a peer. Because the motivation for social interaction is so strong, students will often complete nonpreferred tasks when they can work in pairs or small groups.

- If motivation is a problem, the teacher should determine whether student resistance is associated with motor skills. Because of fine-motor problems, the student often balks at an assignment because the written portion is difficult. Providing a computer for assignment completion or allowing the student to dictate to a peer or into a tape recorder is often enough to prompt the student to begin a task. Some assignments can be modified from an essay to a multiple-choice format to further reduce written requirements. If the teacher is not testing handwriting, there is often little reason to require that an assignment be handwritten.

Hidden Curriculum

Every school has a hidden curriculum—the dos and don'ts that are not spelled out, yet everyone somehow knows about (Bieber, 1994). For example, everyone knows that Mr. Garcia, the English teacher, doesn't really care if you don't turn in your daily assignments, as long as you do well on the end-of-chapter tests. Everyone knows that Mrs. Farquhar, the assistant principal, is a stickler for following the rules, so no one curses or even slouches in her presence. Everyone also knows that the really tough guys (the ones who like to beat up unsuspecting kids) hang out behind the slide, just out of teacher view. Everyone knows these things—that is, everyone except the student with Asperger Syndrome.

Students with Asperger Syndrome are at a disadvantage because they do not understand the hidden curriculum. They inadvertently break the rules associated with the hidden curriculum and either get in trouble with adults or are further ostracized or hurt by peers. As a result, the students require direct instruction on the hidden curriculum. They need to be taught that some middle-school students curse, but none of the students curse in front of an adult, unless that adult is Ms. Stewart, who tends to ignore such things. They need to know that only geeks wear unwashed, unbleached, holeless jeans to school. Understanding the hidden curriculum can make all the difference to students with Asperger Syndrome—it can keep them out of detention and help them make friends.

Who should teach the hidden curriculum? Many teachers voice concern over teaching cetain elements of the culture ("I can't tell them it is all right to curse in front of Ms. Stewart."). However, there are many hidden curriculum elements that teachers can comfortably teach and should teach just as they would reading, writing, or social studies. There are other elements on which teachers should not provide instruction. Peer models can be enlisted to provide this information. However, this should be done carefully. It is recommended that peers identify hidden curriculum elements and then meet to discuss them with teachers and the student's parents. As a group they can decide when, how, and if to provide instruction on these very important elements.

Teacher Interaction Strategies

Parents of these students and adults with Asperger Syndrome have often communicated that individual teachers have made a difference as to whether a particular student was successful in school. They have defined a variety of teacher characteristics that seem to match well with these students' needs. Often these behaviors are not measurable, but involve personality aspects. Overall, these teachers are consistent in the way they structure their classrooms and predictable in the way they act. They tend not to use "top-down management" approaches, allowing the student options whenever possible. This type of teacher understands students with Asperger Syndrome, detecting their stress level and making accommodations as needed. Some additional effective teacher characteristics include the following:

- has a working knowledge of the characteristics of students with Asperger Syndrome
- develops a sense of trust between self and student
- accepts student's cognitive and social abilities and learning potential
- accepts the student as he or she is
- relates to the student's role in school
- enjoys working with the student and voices that enjoyment

- models enjoyment of doing tasks
- indicates that learning is mutual
- works as an unobtrusive facilitator rather than as a dictator
- reacts calmly to all students
- provides nonthreatening feedback
- does not lecture, but provides general direction as needed
- listens to the student, analyzes the student's needs, and adapts curriculum accordingly
- avoids asking "why" questions to understand behavior
- states expected behavior and provides examples
- uses short sentences
- limits the number of instructions that are given at one time
- provides instructions in more than one modality, realizing that visual memory is most often a strength for these students
- uses a flat affect and unemotional tone to redirect the student
- states rules as universals ("Everyone in this class needs to listen when I talk.")
- behaves in a predictable and dependable manner
- provides adequate wait time for the student to process instructions
- provides a classroom structure that is predictable

Concluding Thoughts

Students with Asperger Syndrome, because of their intellectual capabilities, have the potential to be successful in school settings. However, intellectual functioning alone is not enough to ensure that these students have the structure and support they need. Educators must develop environmental modifications and teach strategic skills that these students can use throughout their academic day. Visual, structural, and motivational strategies are integral to these students' success. Just as important to these students' success is selection of a teacher whose characteristics match their needs. Supports must be set into place with careful consideration of how these students' needs can be met.

PLANNING FOR SOCIAL
AND BEHAVIORAL SUCCESS

Children and adolescents with Asperger Syndrome are particularly prone to social peculiarities, social interaction problems and, to a lesser degree, behavioral difficulties. Although they are frequently motivated to be near to and to socially engage peers and adults, children and youth with Asperger Syndrome are deficient in age-appropriate, reciprocal social interaction skills such as those required to participate in cooperative play. These children and youth are often described by others as socially stiff and awkward, emotionally flat, socially unaware, self-absorbed, lacking in empathy, prone to show socially unacceptable behavior, and insensitive or unaware of verbal and nonverbal social cues. Indeed, virtually every educational characteristic of students with Asperger Syndrome is either related or secondary to social skills development. Accordingly, professionals and families must provide specialized support so these children and adolescents can progress and experience success at school and at home. This chapter presents social skills development and behavior management options available to professionals and families.

Social and Behavioral Assessment

The model for assessing children and youth with Asperger Syndrome consists of the same general elements as any thorough assessment for other disabled and nondisabled individuals: (a) Identify and measure at least one behavior to change, (b) analyze the environmental and antecedent factors of the identified behavior or behaviors, and (c) analyze the functions of target behaviors and related behavioral contingencies. Each of these components is discussed as it relates to children and youth with Asperger Syndrome.

Identifying and Measuring Behavior to Change

This step involves specifying the behaviors that need to be modified. Behaviors such as "nonreciprocal social responding," "auditory hypersensitivity," and "sensory and emotional overload" mean different things to different people and therefore are unsuitable as targets for behavioral intervention programs. Instead, target behaviors need to be specified so that they reflect exactly what the behavior is (e.g., one shouldn't say that a child has a problem with auditory hypersensitivity, but rather identify the target behavior as loud screaming). Where and when the behaviors occur is also specified (e.g., loud screaming in any classroom or indoor setting during regular school hours). Such specificity helps adults involved in change programs understand and evaluate interventions. It also enables children with Asperger Syndrome to be knowledgeable and involved participants in program efforts on their behalf.

Baseline behavior data should be regularly and accurately measured. Such measurement continues after a strategy is implemented. Measurement options most appropriate for children and youth with Asperger Syndrome include frequency counts (the number of times a particular behavior is observed), duration assessment (the length of time a behavior lasts), and interval and time sampling. Interval and time sampling involve dividing an observation period into equal time segments and observing whether the target behavior occurs within each segment. Interval sampling requires observation during an entire time segment (e.g., 30 seconds), whereas time sampling requires brief observation of a target response at the end of each segment (e.g., the observer checks if a child is engaged in a particular behavior at the end of each 30-second segment).

Depending on the nature of the targeted behavior and on resource availability, the appropriate measurement procedure is selected. For example, if the target behavior is tantrums, a duration assessment is selected instead of frequency counts, because the length of time a child throws a tantrum is usually more informative than the number of times he throws a tantrum. Similarly, if the target of an intervention program is to reduce the number of times a child is out of her assigned seat during a particular class, frequency counts would likely be most suitable.

Analyzing Environmental and Antecedent Factors

This assessment stage attempts to answer several questions: Is the behavior more likely to occur at certain times, in the presence of certain people, in certain settings or environments, or while a student is working on certain types of assignments? Knowing that a behavior is or is not related to certain factors is of obvious assistance in developing an intervention program. For example, determining that a child primarily engages in argumentative behavior with one paraprofessional suggests possible causes for the behavior, and thus helps in the creation of an intervention program that will probably positively influence the target behavior.

The behavior analysis form shown in Figure 4.1 is designed to assist professionals and parents in better understanding environmental and antecedent factors that may be related to the child's behavior.

Analyzing the Functions and Contingencies of Target Behaviors

Similar to analyzing environmental and antecedent factors connected with a behavior, it is extremely important to analyze the functions and contingencies related to a target behavior when designing effective interventions. Indeed, this program component has received increased attention in recent years, and most professionals now recognize that it is essential to gain a clear understanding of functions of and contributors to target behaviors prior to designing and implementing intervention programs.

Simply speaking, this process involves pinpointing outcomes associated with a child's behavior. For example, critical observations and analysis may reveal that a child seems to act up in the classroom to get her teacher to send her to the school office so she can thus escape an undesired activity. Similarly, careful analysis may reveal that a youth speaks inappropriately in the classroom in an attempt to get adult and peer attention. Parents and professionals equipped with such information have an obvious advantage in developing appropriate and effective intervention programs.

The most effective way of conducting such an analysis is to make direct observation of the individual's behavior in appropriate situations. Thus, if a youth interacts negatively with peers in the school hallways between classes, these interactions would be observed, with special attention to the initiations and responses of the student and his peers and the consequences.

For example, a 16-year-old with Asperger Syndrome routinely begins crying and screaming in the hallway during class breaks. During these periods (four 5-minute breaks), the school psychologist makes the observations shown in Figure 4.2.

The observer has been able to determine that the student routinely goes into the hallway outside his classroom during class breaks and begins asking other students if they are aware of various school rules. This student is well versed in the rules and in fact always carries a copy of the school's disciplinary code. For example, he reminds students that it is against school rules to smoke on school property, and security personnel will be called if somebody is observed smoking. In response to these reminders, his peers have begun intimating that it is acceptable to engage in behaviors identified as unacceptable in the school handbook (e.g., students are allowed to smoke on school property). Confronted with this contradiction, the student with Asperger Syndrome

Name of individual being observed _____

Observer _____

Target behavior observational definition _____

_____

_____

Timing of target behavior

Target behavior primarily occurs:

☐ during structured activities
  Explain: _____

☐ during unstructured activities
  Explain: _____

☐ during lecture times or times of group discussion
  Explain: _____

☐ when working or playing with others
  Explain: _____

☐ when working or playing alone
  Explain: _____

☐ during free time
  Explain: _____

☐ during times of transition
  Explain: _____

☐ primarily during morning hours
  Explain: _____

☐ primarily during afternoon hours
  Explain: _____

☐ in specific environments (e.g., classroom, lunchroom, gym)
  Explain: _____

☐ other
  Explain: _____

Figure 4.1. Environmental and antecedent analysis form

Relation of target behavior to the presence of others

Target behavior primarily occurs:

☐ when working or playing with another student at school
    ☐ specific peer
    ☐ all peers
    Explain: _____

☐ when working or playing with a sibling or peer at home or in community
    ☐ specific sibling
    ☐ all siblings
    ☐ specific peer
    ☐ all peers
    Explain: _____

☐ when working or interacting with an adult at school
    ☐ specific adult
    ☐ all adults
    Explain: _____

☐ when working or interacting with a parent or other adult at home or in community
    ☐ specific parent
    ☐ both parents
    ☐ specific adult
    ☐ all adults
    Explain: _____

☐ while a student is working on certain types of assignments
    Explain: _____

*Summary analysis of timing of target behavior, presence of others,
and other correlates of target behavior*

_____

_____

_____

_____

_____

_____

Figure 4.1. Continued.

Time	Setting	Task	Behavior (B), consequence (C), and response (R) analysis
8:55–9:00	hallway outside class (class break)	none	B: Target student approaches group of students to remind them of school rules. Begins reading various school rules and consequences for infractions.
			C: Peers ignore student; one peer tells student to go away.
			R: Target student retreats and reads class rule book.
			B: Target student repeats rules; reminds peers that security personnel may be called to enforce rules.
			C: Peer informs student that rules don't apply to them: "Mr. Walker [principal] says it's OK to smoke in school."
			R: Target student attempts to show peer the written rule. When peer refuses to look at rule book and indicates that security personnel are being sent, student begins to cry and scream and continues until quieted by a teacher assigned to patrol hallways.

Figure 4.2. Functional analysis observation example

tries to show his peers the written rule, but they indicate that they will call security personnel to "arrest" the student. The student consequently becomes upset and starts crying and screaming, much to the delight of his peers. Prompted by the crying and screaming, teachers or administrators attempt to calm or discipline the student.

Use of a functional analysis method such as the one shown in Figure 4.2 does not guarantee an effective intervention program. However, a functional analysis is an efficient and effective tool for understanding variables and outcomes related to students' problems, and for designing and implementing appropriate intervention programs.

Structuring the Environment for Social Success

It is clear that children and youth with Asperger Syndrome do not learn social behaviors in the same fashion as their nondisabled peers. That is, they do not spontaneously and incidentally learn myriad and highly complex social responses, almost all of which vary at least slightly from situation to situation. For instance, beginning at a young age, children are expected to discriminate among situations when it is appropriate to talk to and interact with other children (e.g., during recess as opposed to classroom "quiet time") and to select conversational topics that correspond to various situations, circumstances, and shared interests. Thus, a child waiting in line with peers for her turn in a game of kick-ball is more likely to experience a positive peer response to a conversation about the ball game or similar activity than to a conversation about an unrelated, narrowly defined topic in which other students have little or no interest.

Without assistance, most children and youth with Asperger Syndrome will display a variety of socially incorrect, unaccepted, and nonreciprocal behaviors. Moreover, without support these individuals are vulnerable to emotional stress and apt to become agitated by social situations that they misinterpret. Structure for children with Asperger Syndrome minimizes their being teased, bullied, or taken advantage of by peers.

There are no universally effective methods for structuring environments and situations for children with Asperger Syndrome. Nevertheless, these children generally benefit from predictable environments. The security that comes from being able to anticipate and understand activities, schedules, and expectations helps these children remain calm and enables them to appropriately meet various classroom, home, and community demands. Procedures that are helpful in creating such structure include (a) establishing clear expectations and rules for social behavior; (b) creating routines and schedules; and (c) making physical, environmental, cognitive, and attitudinal support available.

Expectations and Rules

Use of clear expectations for social and behavioral performance is one of the more effective and efficient means of establishing structure for children with Asperger Syndrome. The importance of such expectations to these children's social and behavioral success is obvious: Children and youth with Asperger Syndrome routinely experience difficulty understanding expectations and consequences. Accordingly, adults involved with these children must clearly and explicitly state, model, and illustrate rules, including desired behaviors. That is, children with Asperger Syndrome should not only be instructed in what not to do but also in acceptable behaviors. For example, students should not exclusively be told that they are not permitted to play in the unfenced area next to the school where the teachers' cars are parked. Rather, they should be instructed that they are permitted to play in the paved, fenced area around the school. Without such specificity it cannot be assumed that children with Asperger Syndrome will understand and be able to follow rules.

Rules established for these children should also be utilitarian. Although this suggestion has obvious relevance for all children, it appears to be particularly important for children and youth with Asperger Syndrome. "Rule-related functional value" refers to establishing and enforcing rules that clearly and deliberately reinforce and facilitate students' social and cognitive development. For instance, adults should not establish rules that are designed to exclusively develop children's compliance or establish that the adults are "in charge," but otherwise have no functional value.

Also, rules and expectations should be regularly reviewed, and children should practice following rules by rehearsing desired classroom, home, and community behaviors and simulating potentially problematic situations. Finally, adults should closely monitor rules, maintain consistent expectations, and consistently apply consequences.

Expectations can be clarified by incorporating reviews of classroom and home expectations and rules into daily routines. For example, an adult should briefly review playground rules prior to recess or grocery store behavior prior to entering the store. Classroom and school rules and expectations should be presented visually, such as on bulletin board posters that identify appropriate recess games and activities. Below is an example of how rules relating to reading during free time were presented in one classroom.

▶ **During Free Reading Time:**

Choose a book or magazine to read.
You may read anywhere in the room.
You may read with a friend.
You must read quietly.
When the timer goes off, quietly return to your desk.

(Example by Valerie Janke Rexin)

Another means of helping children understand and follow rules is for adults to identify cues or use physical prompts that alert students that their behavior is unacceptable. For example, a teacher may indicate that he will hold up a clipboard when he observes a child failing to take her turn in a game during recess. In this scenario, the student would rehearse coming to the teacher for instruction on appropriate play behavior whenever she observed her teacher holding a clipboard above his head.

Routines and Schedules

Routines and schedules can also provide structure for children and youth with Asperger Syndrome, building on their preference for predictability, order, and consistency. The vast majority of nondisabled children and youth are able to effectively respond to environmental variables and to adapt to their ever-changing world. In contrast, children and youth with Asperger Syndrome tend to focus on only certain environmental variables and to have strong negative reactions to environmental changes. For example, a youth may fail to respond to information heard over the school intercom system. Other children with Asperger Syndrome may become extremely upset when classroom schedules are adjusted to accommodate a school-wide assembly or to respond to inclement weather.

It should be noted that even though resistance to change is a common characteristic of individuals with Asperger Syndrome, it is neither possible nor desirable to follow a routine without deviation. Nonetheless, it is important to recognize that many individuals with Asperger Syndrome have a strong preference for routine and consistency. Thus, teachers, families, and others who are in regular contact with these children would be wise to establish and follow predictable routines and to prepare the children in advance of anticipated changes. For example, after discussing the situation, a parent may follow an alternate route to school. Although such a deviation may seem trivial, it may be significant for a child with Asperger Syndrome.

Thus, it is important to build on preferences for routine and consistency while introducing strategies to help children deal with change, because learning to adjust to change has obvious implications for the well-being and development of individuals with Asperger Syndrome. Group and individual schedules presented in written, pictorial, or combination format (see example below and in Chapter 3) are useful in communicating the sequence of daily activities and in alerting children to new activities and schedule deviations.

▶ **Travis's Wednesday Schedule**

8:15–8:30	group time
8:35–9:20	English
9:25–10:10	history
10:15–11:00	study hall
11:05–11:50	math
11:55–12:30	lunch
12:35–1:20	music
1:25–2:20	P.E.
2:25–3:10	resource room
3:15–3:30	group time
3:30	leave for home

(Example by Valerie Janke Rexin)

Physical, Environmental, Cognitive, and Attitudinal Support

This type of support relates to having adequate resources to effectively sustain, manage, and supervise children and youth with Asperger Syndrome in various settings, including classrooms and other school settings such as play areas and lunchrooms; home settings; and community settings such as shopping centers, churches, and recreational sites.

Above and beyond all other resources, it is essential that children and youth with Asperger Syndrome associate with adults and peers who are knowledgeable about the disorder, aware of individual needs, and capable of creating environments and situations to support these needs. It is essential that children with Asperger Syndrome have the support of parents, family members, peers, teachers, and other support personnel (e.g., psychologists, speech pathologists, paraprofessionals) who are knowledgeable and skilled in understanding and working with persons with Asperger Syndrome. In far too many instances, peers have bullied and provoked children with Asperger Syndrome to engage in inappropriate behaviors out of ignorance. Accordingly, one major step in preparing supportive environments for these children is to inform their peers and teachers of the nature of the disorder and their role in supporting these children.

Social Interventions

Professionals and parents alike consider social interaction opportunities and social skills development to be essential for children and youth with Asperger Syndrome. Yet, as previously observed, these areas tend to be problematic. Accordingly, increasing the quantity and quality of social interactions for children with Asperger Syndrome is of paramount concern. Although this is in no way an easy process, certain methods have proven very effective, including social stories, social scripts, Situation Options Consequences Choices Strategies Simulation (SOCCSS), social autopsies, direct instruction, and adult- and peer-mediated strategies.

Social Stories

Because of their relatively strong cognitive and language skills, children and adolescents with Asperger Syndrome often benefit from the structure imposed by self-instructional and self-control problem-solving procedures. That is, they are often able to positively respond to strategies based on directives and guidance for responding to various situations. One of the most promising of these options is social stories (Gray & Gerard, 1993; Swaggart et al., 1995). A social story describes social situations specific to individuals and circumstances. For instance, a social story might be developed for a youth who attends a general education English class. In the story, there is a description of the youth, the setting, peers and adults associated with the setting, and the youth's feelings and perceptions related to the setting (e.g., the youth likes to read and write in his class journal). There are also directive statements that describe appropriate behaviors for the setting (e.g., upon entering the classroom the youth should sit at his desk and take out his textbook, and until the bell rings he may quietly talk to people seated near him). Thus, this method involves structuring an individual's behavior and social responses by offering individualized, specific response cues. Although the empirical efficacy of social stories has not been definitively established, preliminary indications are that it may be a beneficial method of offering structure for many children and youth with Asperger Syndrome. Shown below is an example of a social story for a child with Asperger Syndrome.

▶ Social Story Related to Lunch Behavior

Every day I look forward to lunch. Lunch is a time I get to eat and to be with other children in Ms. Zenith's class. At 12 noon Ms. Zenith announces that it is time to get ready for lunch. When she tells me, I get my lunch from my locker and walk to the cafeteria. Sometimes the cafeteria is noisy. I can sit at any table during lunch time. I like to sit with my friends. When I am finished with my lunch, I throw away my trash. When the bell rings, I go back to my locker and get ready for my next class.

(Example by Valerie Janke Rexin)

Table 4.1 provides guidelines for structuring a social story for a child with Asperger Syndrome.

Social Scripts

Children and youth with Asperger Syndrome may also benefit from having adults structure their behaviors through the use of scripts. For instance, a child and his teacher may practice a script for joining in a group game at recess. This option minimizes problems these children have with being able to spontaneously generate language and deal with the complexity of deciding how to approach peers. Moreover, when paired with peer interaction training (i.e., direct instruction and adult- and peer-mediated strategies), it provides a structured interactive routine that facilitates predictable responses.

Situation Options Consequences Choices Strategies Simulation

The Situation Options Consequences Choices Strategies Simulation (SOCCSS) strategy was developed to help students with social interaction problems put interpersonal relationships into a sequential form (J. Roosa, personal communication, June 4, 1997). It helps students understand problem situations and lets them see that they have to make choices about a given situation, with each choice having a consequence. The SOCCSS strategy works as follows:

1. *Situation.* When a social problem arises, the teacher works with the student to identify the situation. Specifically, they identify (a) who was involved; (b) what happened; (c) the date, day, and time of occurrence; and (d) reasons for the present situation. Together they define the problem and state a goal through discussion, writing, and drawings.

2. *Options.* Following identification of the situation, the student and teacher brainstorm several options for behavior. At this point, the teacher accepts all student responses and does not evaluate them. Typically, the options are listed in written or

Table 4.1
Guidelines for Social Story Construction

---

1. Identify a target behavior or problem situation for social story intervention.

The educator should select a social behavior to be changed, preferably one whose improvement can result in increased positive social interactions, a safer environment, additional social learning opportunities, or all three. The behavior should be broken down into its component parts and based on the student's ability level. For example, during lunch Bob grabs food from his peers' plates and eats it. He exhibits this behavior at school, home, and restaurants. People who do not know Bob often react in a hostile manner. Accordingly, grabbing food from other people's plates is targeted for modification because it is socially unacceptable and interferes with development of more acceptable social contacts.

2. Define target behavior for data collection.

For several reasons, it is imperative to clearly define the behavior on which data will be collected. First, all data collectors need an identical understanding of the targeted behavior to ensure reliability in measuring change. In addition, the behavior should be defined in such a way that the student understands the behavior to be exhibited. For example, Bob's current eating behavior consists of eating and grabbing. *Eating* is defined as sitting and consuming food only from the plate that is in front of him. *Grabbing* is defined as removing food from a plate other than his own.

3. Collect baseline data on the target behavior.

Collecting data over an extended period allows the educator to determine a trend. Baseline data collection can last from 3 to 5 days or longer. To measure Bob's food-grabbing behavior, the observer can place a tally mark on a sheet of paper each time Bob grabs food from a peer's plate during lunch. The observer then logs the total number of tally marks onto a separate sheet of paper with the corresponding date.

4. Write a short social story using descriptive, directive, and perspective sentences.

A good rule of thumb for writing social stories is to use descriptive and perspective sentences for every directive sentence in the story (Gray, 1994). Stories should be written in accordance with the student's comprehension skills, with vocabulary and print size individualized for each student. The stories should be written in the first person and in present or future tense (to describe a situation as it occurs or to anticipate an upcoming event, respectively).

5. Choose the number of sentences per page according to the student's functioning level.

Presentation of the social story is dependent on the student's functioning level. For some students, one to three sentences per page is adequate. Each sentence allows the student to focus on and process a specific concept. Depending on the student's skill level, more than one sentence per page may result in an overload of information such that the student does not comprehend the information.

(continues)

Table 4.1 *Continued.*

6. Use photographs, hand-drawn pictures, or pictorial icons.

Pictures may enhance student understanding of appropriate behavior, especially with students who lack reading skills. For example, icons have been shown to be effective learning tools for children and youth. Gray (1994), however, cautioned that illustrations may too narrowly define a situation, resulting in limited generalization. Thus, decisions about whether to use pictures with social stories should be made on an individual basis. A picture on Bob's social story might depict him eating appropriately.

7. Read the social story to the student and model the desired behavior.

Reading the social story and modeling related behaviors as needed should become a consistent part of the student's daily schedule. For example, the story may be read just prior to the activity targeted by the story. Accordingly, Bob's story might be read to him right before lunch or at the beginning of the day to help him anticipate the situation and appropriate behavior. Depending on the student's functioning level, the teacher or the student may read the story. The student who is able to read independently may read the social story to peers so that all have a similar perspective of the targeted situation and appropriate behaviors.

8. Collect intervention data.

The educator should collect data throughout the social story program, using the procedures described for collecting and analyzing baseline data.

9. Review the findings and related social story procedures.

If the student does not respond with the desired behavior after 2 weeks of the social story program, the educator should review the social story and its implementation procedures. It is recommended that if program alterations are made, only one variable should be changed at a time (e.g., change only the content of the story, rather than simultaneously changing the time the story is read and the person who reads it). By changing only one factor at a time, the educator can determine the factor or factors that best facilitate a student's learning. For example, changing the time that Bob's food-grabbing social story is presented, from just before lunch to earlier in the morning, may allow him to reflect on appropriate behaviors and thus improve the program. On the other hand, if the time and the story content were changed at the same time, the teacher would be unsure of which factor was responsible for Bob's behavior change.

10. Program for maintenance and generalization.

After a behavior change has become consistent, the educator may want to fade use of the social story. Fading may be accomplished by extending the time between readings or having students be responsible for reading the story themselves. By their very nature social stories permit generalization across environments. Thus, teachers should assist students in applying social story content to various situations. For example, the teacher could assist Bob in using his appropriate eating skills during snack time, at parties, and in restaurants. In addition, the teacher should ensure that the student continues the appropriate behavior. Finally, students with sufficient independent skills may be assisted in identifying social goals for which they may develop their own social stories.

pictorial format. According to Spivack, Platt, and Shure (1976), this step is critical to problem solving. The ability to generate multiple solutions diminishes student frustration, encourages the student to see more than one perspective, and results in student resiliency.

3. *Consequences.* The student and teacher work together to evaluate each of the options generated. Kaplan and Carter (1995) suggest that each of the options be evaluated using the following criteria: (a) efficacy—Will the solution get me what I want? and (b) feasibility—Will I be able to do it? Each of the consequences is labeled with an E for efficacy or F for feasibility. The teacher works as a facilitator, helping the student to develop consequences for each option without dictating consequences. The teacher uses pointed questions to help the student develop his or her own consequences.

4. *Choices.* During this stage, the student selects the option or options that will have the most desirable consequences.

5. *Strategy.* A planned action is developed by the student and teacher. The plan should be generated by the student to facilitate ownership. The teacher should ask questions that lead the student into developing an effective plan.

6. *Simulation.* Finally, the student is given an opportunity to role-play the solution. Simulation could occur in the following ways: (a) find a quiet place to image how the strategy will work, (b) talk with a peer about the plan of action, (c) write down on paper what may occur when the strategy is implemented, and (d) practice or role-play with one or more people the strategy developed to address the problem.

Social Autopsies

Social autopsies were developed by Richard LaVoie (Bieber, 1994) to help students with severe learning and social problems develop an understanding of social mistakes. An autopsy, in the traditional sense, is the examination and inspection of a dead body to discover the cause of death, determine damage, and prevent reoccurrence. A social autopsy is an examination and inspection of a social error to discover the cause of the error, determine the damage, and prevent it from occurring again. When a social mistake occurs, the student meets with an educator or caregiver to discuss it. Together, in a nonpunitive fashion, they identify the mistake. They then discuss who was harmed by the error. The third step of the autopsy is development of a plan to ensure that the error does not occur again. Because of the visual strengths, problem-solving deficits, and language processing problems of children with Asperger Syndrome, social autopsies may be enhanced by using written words or phrases or pictures to illustrate each of the steps.

Direct Instruction

Relative to increasing the quantity and quality of peer interactions and developing social skills, direct instruction refers to directly guiding children in desired responses. Thus, the first step in direct instruction is identifying the social interaction or social skill goal or goals (e.g., playing a cooperative, age-appropriate board game with a peer). Second, the steps the child takes to reach the goal are identified (e.g., approach a peer with an invitation to play, obtain the game from its designated storage space, ask the peer to choose a color for game pieces, and so forth). Third, these steps are sequentially taught to the child using best practices methods. Such methods include modeling (e.g., demonstrating the desired social behavior related to a cooperative board game), providing multiple opportunities to practice desired behaviors (e.g., allowing the child to practice playing the board game with teachers and others before playing the game with peers), providing instructional prompts (e.g., prompting the child to drop dice on the board and move his or her game piece the correct number of spaces), reinforcing desired behaviors (e.g., praising the child for cooperatively playing the game with a peer), and providing multiple opportunities to engage in the desired behavior (e.g., giving the child opportunities to play board games with different peers at different times of the day).

An example of direct instruction on participating in a group leisure activity is shown below.

▶ **Direct Instruction of a Leisure Skill**

In an effort to develop a social activity in which Alex could participate during recess, Mr. Goldberg selected "four-square," an activity Alex and his classmates enjoyed and commonly participated in. Mr. Goldberg task-analyzed the skills needed by Alex to participate in this activity: (a) Identify one or more partners, (b) request that they join in playing four-square, (c) follow rules of the game (e.g., "play fair," take turns), and (d) put away materials when directed by a teacher or at the conclusion of recess. Mr. Goldberg then taught the skills to Alex, first by modeling them and then by asking Alex to role-play the steps with him. Next, he gave Alex opportunities to practice the new skills with different peers and teachers. During this time, Mr. Goldberg provided prompts and reinforcement to Alex as needed, thus ensuring that he had multiple opportunities to use these new skills during various recess periods.

(Example by Valerie Janke Rexin)

A primary advantage of direct instruction is that it is based on methods that have been empirically shown to have social validity. The primary disadvantage is that direct instruction of social interaction skills does not always generalize to other settings and situations. That is, a child who is taught to play a particular board game with a limited number of students in her classroom may show little interest in playing similar games or engaging in alternative peer activities, playing with new children, or engaging in the desired behavior outside her classroom. Thus, social skills training based on direct instruction must be geared to respond to these potential problems.

Adult-Mediated Strategies

Adult-mediated strategies involve two basic procedures. First, the child or youth with Asperger Syndrome is paired with a socially desirable age peer in a setting supportive of social interaction. In this context, "socially desirable" refers to a child who is willing and able to follow directions, engage in desired social behaviors, and model appropriate social responses. The identified peer (or peers) is instructed to remain close to the child with Asperger Syndrome during specified times such as recess, classroom free time, and so forth. The peer is also instructed to be prepared to participate in a game or activity with the child if the child initiates or otherwise indicates interest in engaging in social interaction.

To facilitate social interactions between the child with Asperger Syndrome and the designated peer, an adult (e.g., classroom teacher, school paraprofessional) remains close to the child and provides verbal prompts. For instance, a teacher may prompt a child to approach a peer who has been coached to be receptive to playing a game or sharing an activity. If the child with Asperger Syndrome complies with the prompt, his or her behavior is reinforced by the adult. If the child fails to follow the adult's prompt, the directive is repeated, and when appropriate, the adult physically assists the child in following the prompt. An example of an adult-mediated strategy is shown below.

▶ Adult-Mediated Instruction of a Free-Period Activity

During free periods, Ms. Rodriguez, a third-grade teacher, notices that Angela is not engaged in an activity. Ms. Rodriguez prompts Angela to ask another student to participate in an activity such as playing a computer game. Based on this prompt, Angela approaches a peer and asks if she would like to play "Family Feud" on the computer. The peer agrees to play a computer game; however, she indicates a desire to play a different game. In response, Ms. Rodriguez prompts Angela to offer a list of choices to her peer. When the students mutually agree on a computer game and begin to play, the teacher stays close by. Ms. Rodriguez praises Angela for her playing techniques and prompts her as needed.

(*Example by Valerie Janke Rexin*)

There is little doubt that adult-mediated social interaction programs can be effective. Adult-mediated strategies can be (a) used to develop a variety of social skills in a variety of settings, (b) used with groups of children, and (c) generalized through careful planning. Disadvantages of adult-mediated strategies should also be considered when planning social interaction programs; the most distinct disadvantage is that adult-mediated strategies may disrupt natural and ongoing peer social exchanges. That is, the presence of an adult in an ongoing peer exchange is unnatural and may interfere with reciprocal interactions. For instance, a child with Asperger Syndrome may constantly seek support and guidance from an adult and only respond when prompted. Moreover, when the child with Asperger Syndrome does respond, the adult mediation may further the development of stiff, unnatural interactions. In spite of these potential problems, adult-mediated strategies have been found to be among the most effective ways of increasing social interactions.

Peer-Mediated Strategies

Peer-mediated strategies involve socially competent peers who are taught to initiate and support social interactions with children and youth with Asperger Syndrome. Following such training, these individuals are placed in social situations where they participate in social activities with the children and youth with Asperger Syndrome. Unlike adult-mediated strategies, no adults provide social interaction prompts. Rather, after training, children with Asperger Syndrome and their peers participate in social activities independent of direct adult involvement.

This strategy has been associated with an increase in positive, appropriate behaviors of individuals with disabilities, which in turn promotes peer acceptance. There is some indication that peer-mediated strategies are most effective when popular, high-status peers serve as confederates. Use of groups composed of two peers and one child with Asperger Syndrome has also been advocated by some researchers as a means of obtaining higher levels of social interaction and promoting more normal social interaction patterns. An example of a peer-mediated strategy is shown below.

▶ Peer-Mediated Activity

Miss Simmons decides to adopt a peer-mediated strategy to increase social interactions between Latanya and her classmates. This decision is based on Miss Simmons' observation that Latanya is consistently isolated from her peers during recess, free time, and lunch periods. Prior to selecting an appropriate peer, she identifies a classmate whom she observes occasionally talks to and plays with Latanya. Based on this observation, Miss Simmons invites the peer to participate in a social interaction enhancement program. Upon the peer's acceptance, Miss Simmons trains Latanya and the peer to interact during a variety of activities, including how the peer should respond to Latanya's invitations to play, prompting procedures, and reinforcement methods. Subsequent to peer training, Miss Simmons observes the students, makes suggestions, and offers feedback as needed. However, during the social activity itself, she allows Latanya and her peer to independently interact.

(Example by Valerie Janke Rexin)

There are a number of advantages to using peer-mediated strategies. First, this approach is the most natural means of promoting socialization, as it relies on naturally occurring interactions between peers. After initial training, adults permit children to socialize, thus ensuring that activities are based on normally occurring social interactions and on behaviors of socially competent peers rather than on artificial or simulated scenarios. Peer-mediated strategies are relatively easy to implement and typically offer the best results in terms of quantity and quality of social interaction.

Weaknesses of peer-mediated strategies include the question of whether social interaction skills will be generalized to other peers, environments, and situations, because the children are trained to work with designated peers in their classroom on certain activities. There is also a question of whether skills developed by children through peer-mediated strategies will be maintained over time.

Additional Suggestions for Promoting Social Interactions

Without question, children and youth with Asperger Syndrome benefit from social interaction training. However, different children have different needs, and different situations call for different programs. Thus, it is likely that social interaction programs will prove to be useful at least with certain individuals and in certain situations.

The success of social interaction programs may be enhanced by careful consideration of other factors:

- Adults associated with children and youth with Asperger Syndrome must carefully and collaboratively establish appropriate social interaction goals. It is not appropriate or reasonable to expect that these children will become socially skilled and sophisticated as a result of any intervention program. Thus, while reasonable improvements can be expected, it is highly unlikely that the strategies discussed in this section will produce a "cure."

- Adults involved in designing and implementing social interaction programs for children and youth with Asperger Syndrome should design their programs to coincide with existing social interaction activities and opportunities, as opposed to creating entirely new situations.

- Social interaction programs should be designed to allow for the fact that these programs require both initial and ongoing training and support. It is unreasonable to expect that once a program is initiated, it will effectively continue without ongoing support.

- Social interaction programs should include plans for skill generalization and maintenance.

Behavior Interventions

Support for children and youth with Asperger Syndrome can also come in the form of behavior interventions that are compatible with these children's unique social characteristics. In this regard, the uniqueness of children and youth with Asperger Syndrome warrants particular attention. These children require behavior intervention strategies that do not use a typical top-down approach. Strategies that work best with this population include those in which students have an interest, investment, and choice. It is strongly recommended that children with Asperger Syndrome be involved in program development and implementation. Such participation increases their understanding of rules, expectations, and consequences and increases the chance that they will be proactive in program implementation and evaluation.

Cognitive Behavior Modification

Cognitive behavior modification (CBM) is a technique that teaches individuals to monitor their own behavior, pace, or performance and to deliver self-reinforcement at established intervals. In this strategy, the locus of behavior control is shifted from an external source, such as a teacher or supervisor, to the individual. Cognitive behavior modification can be used to facilitate a variety of behavior changes, from task completion to on-task behavior in either school or work settings. The procedure is most appropriate for students who have the necessary skills to independently perform a particular task, but are unable to complete it because of attention difficulties. It is not appropriate for the student who does not possess the skills necessary to complete assigned work. The six steps required for implementing cognitive behavior modification are detailed in Table 4.2.

Reinforcers

Reinforcers are interventions that increase the occurrence of a desired behavior, by following a desired behavior with either a positive consequence or the removal of an unpleasant stimulus. For obvious reasons, the latter option is less preferred. Based on a thorough environmental and functional analysis of behavior, three forms of positive reinforcement have particular utility with children and youth with Asperger Syndrome: contingent activities, social consequences, and token economy systems (see Table 4.3).

As previously suggested, reinforcement programs may be best implemented through collaborative social contracts wherein adults and students with Asperger Syndrome clearly define goals, expectations, and consequences. Students should receive reinforcers that are extremely powerful and motivating. Reinforcers should be offered in menus from which the student may select. Menus should be rotated frequently to ensure that students do not become sated on a particular reinforcer. These programs are frequently most effective when the students are permitted to apply them through self-management and other cognitive-based methods.

Behavior Contracts

Behavior contracts or contingency contracts offer the teacher and the student with Asperger Syndrome a flexible means of addressing individual needs. For example, a contract may be used to teach new behaviors, maintain existing behaviors, extinguish undesirable behaviors, or provide enrichment opportunities. A behavior contract is an agreement among parties (e.g., teacher, student, parents) that specific behaviors will result in specific consequences. The contract focuses on positive outcomes, and skills and consequences (typically in the form of reinforcement menus) are stated in a manner that leads the student to success. Downing (1990) outlined the steps needed to develop, implement, and monitor a behavior contract. These guidelines are listed in Table 4.4.

Table 4.2
Steps for Implementing a Cognitive Behavior Modification Program

1. Pre-training preparation

Target the problem area. The first step in implementing a cognitive behavior modification (CBM) training program is to identify the problem behavior. It is recommended that only one behavior be targeted at any one time. Target behaviors typically fall into three classes: (a) behaviors that need to be decreased (i.e., those that are disruptive, distracting, or dangerous to self and others), (b) behaviors that need to be increased (i.e., those the student performs 60–80% of the time with teacher assistance), and (c) behaviors that need to be maintained (i.e., those the student performs at least 80% of the time without teacher assistance). One of the most important goals is to target a behavior that a person exhibits on some level and increase either the frequency or quality of the behavior.

The student should actively participate in targeting a behavior for change. The teacher and student should jointly discuss and define the inappropriate and appropriate behaviors. However, the teacher should first have a general idea of the behavior to be changed. In addition, the teacher should be prepared to define the behavior so that it is meaningful to the student.

Identify reinforcers. The CBM strategy is more successful if student preferences for reinforcers are used. The teacher must decide which types of reinforcement will accompany CBM, the frequency with which the reinforcement will occur, and how it will be faded. Although three types of reinforcement can be used (social, contingent activities, tangible/edible), teachers should emphasize the use of higher level reinforcers, particularly those that are social in nature.

Prepare materials. Three items must be prepared: a timing device, a data collection sheet, and self-management tools. The creation, organization, and use of the materials should be practical so that they will be easy to use for both the student and the teacher. Materials should also be selected based on student preference.

Timing devices such as an audiotape or wristwatch can be used to designate time intervals. The length of the intervals should be commensurate with student attention to task. A timing signal will cue the student that it is time to document behavior. For example, if a student can stay on task for approximately 10 minutes, the signal should occur at 10-minute intervals. The student may require instruction on how to use the timing device.

A data collection sheet is used to monitor student progress and to determine strategy effectiveness. The type of data collection sheet used depends on the type of data collected. For example, frequency data will allow teachers to measure the number of intervals the student was on task. Duration data can be used to measure the amount of time in minutes that a behavior occurs. The teacher may elect to synthesize student progress on a graph. This provides a visual representation of the student's progress based on the data collected. The student might also keep a bar graph showing on-task behavior.

The type of self-management tool is dependent on the student's functioning level and the task. The student may use a self-monitoring sheet that resembles other seatwork materials to record on-task behavior. The teacher and student should clearly design materials and discuss their use so that they can be consistently and accurately used.

(continues)

Table 4.2 *Continued.*

2. Discrimination training

The discrimination training component assists students in becoming aware of their own behavior and how it impacts learning and successful task completion. During this stage, the student is taught to distinguish appropriate and inappropriate behavior, as well as incomplete and complete tasks. Instructional methods for use during discrimination training include: videotaping, picture cues, direct teaching, modeling, verbal feedback, and physical guidance through the task. Because many students with Asperger Syndrome are not aware of how their behaviors affect task completion, it is important to provide them with a concrete representation.

Videotaping the student during the same classroom period that the CBM strategy will be used is an effective way to promote self-awareness. A 15-minute sample of seatwork behavior is generally sufficient for use during the discrimination training session. If data are being collected to document behavior change, a minimum of 5 days of videotape should be taken. This serves as baseline data. The videotape helps the student realize relationships, such as that between off-task behavior and failure to complete assigned work. The student is presented with concrete evidence of off-task behavior, thereby helping the student gain a clear perception of actual behavior without allowing denial mechanisms to cloud the issue. However, care should be taken to prevent this step from being viewed as punitive. The positive aspects of on-task behavior should be emphasized.

The teacher then introduces CBM, explaining that this strategy will help the student increase on-task behavior and task completion. The teacher and student view the videotape of student performance, discussing the student's feelings about behaviors seen on the tape. The student then identifies three specific on-task and three specific off-task behaviors seen on the tape and records them on a seatwork behavior chart. Finally, the teacher and student work together to define a specific criterion for target behavior occurrence. Often, students with Asperger Syndrome initially suggest that they be held to 100% accuracy for all sessions. However, this is not realistic for most tasks. The teacher should guide the student to select a reasonable criterion. The student may be directed to observe the behavior of another student to develop this goal.

3. Self-management implementation

During self-management implementation, the teacher explains the CBM strategy. The student will learn through receiving a rationale, as well as through direct instruction, modeling, and guided practice. Self-management implementation depends on the method used, as well as on the student and his or her abilities, because each person learns at a different rate. Thus, what may take one person a few weeks to master may take another person a month.

The teacher instructs the student on the following steps:

a. *Self-monitoring.* The student listens to the timing signal. When the student hears the signal, he or she will question, "Am I paying attention?"

b. *Self-recording.* The student quickly assesses if he or she was attending. If the student was attending, he or she will circle "yes" on the self-monitoring sheet. If the student was off-task, he or she will circle "no" on the self-monitoring sheet.

c. *Self-rewarding.* The student rewards himself or herself for on-task behavior by saying, "Good job." If the student was off-task, he or she will silently prompt, "Get back to work." The student resumes work immediately.

(continues)

Table 4.2 *Continued.*

The teacher models these three steps using the videotape that was prepared earlier. The teacher views the videotape with the student and models the self-monitoring process by listening for the timing signal, stopping the videotape when it is heard, and asking, "Is (student's name) paying attention?" The teacher then verbalizes the answer and marks the appropriate answer on the self-monitoring sheet. Finally, the teacher models the use of the reward or prompting statement.

After the teacher has modeled the strategy for several minutes, the student attempts to self-monitor while viewing the videotape. Initially, it will be necessary for the teacher to direct the process and give assistance to the student. During this step of the training, it is important that the student use overt speech, that is, vocalize the self-assessment, reward, and prompting statements out loud.

4. Self-management independence training

The student practices the strategy under teacher direction, beginning with overt speech and fading to covert speech. The session begins with a review of on- and off-task behaviors, purpose (to stay on task), and goal of the strategy (to complete assigned work during seatwork time and self-monitor behavior). The steps to be followed during the process (self-monitoring, self-recording, and self-rewarding) are also reviewed. Finally, the student discusses the strategy aloud using the videotape, timing signal, and self-monitoring sheet. The student continues this process with overt speech until the process has become routine and the student is using it accurately. When the student follows the process correctly, he is instructed to fade overt speech to whispering, then to covert or silent speech. The teacher provides continuous feedback on student progress.

At this point, the student no longer self-monitors on-task behavior on videotape, but uses the strategy during seatwork time. The timing device and self-monitoring sheet are placed on the student's desk. The teacher may elect to continue to videotape seatwork for 3 to 5 days to allow the student to see progress. In addition, the teacher collects daily data on student behavior to establish strategy efficacy. The teacher may choose to discontinue daily data collection when the strategy appears to be working. However, the teacher continues to monitor that the student is using the strategy correctly and maintaining on-task behavior.

5. Treatment withdrawal

The ultimate goal of this strategy is to allow the student to independently engage in the targeted behavior at an acceptable rate. Thus, for this strategy to be deemed initially effective, both the teacher and the CBM materials should be faded. Fading should be done with the same careful consideration that went into the initial stages of discrimination training, self-management implementation, and self-management independence training. It is imperative that the student be able to initiate and complete the strategy without teacher assistance. The teacher continuously monitors the targeted behavior after the trainer and materials are removed. An increase in inappropriate behavior requires reevaluation and readjustment of the withdrawal process. Student readiness for generalization is also evaluated.

6. Generalization training

Generalization training allows the student to self-monitor the targeted behavior across different subject areas, activities, classrooms, or all three. In addition, it may help the student to target other, similar behaviors for which the strategy may be appropriate. Instruction at this stage assumes the same degree of importance as in the training phase. Unless the student is taught to use and modify the strategy as needed, lasting behavior change has not occurred.

Table 4.3
Types of Reinforcers

Reinforcer	Description
Contingent activities	This reinforcer makes certain preferred events (e.g., computer time) contingent on an individual's satisfactorily meeting some previously specified level of performance or behavior. For instance, after meeting a prescribed standard of academic work and behavior, a child might be permitted to work on a puzzle in the free-time area of his classroom. Children and youth with Asperger Syndrome often have strong (albeit sometimes peculiar) preferences for free time, and frequently benefit from the structure inherent in following adult-directed activities with preferred activities, which makes this a particularly effective tool.
Social consequences	Adults and peers offer contingent, supportive, and constructive verbal and nonverbal feedback. This tool is powerful if the student with Asperger Syndrome understands the social behavior being communicated and the reason why it is being communicated. Social consequences must be overtly used with careful definitions so that the student can interpret them correctly. This can be one of the most effective ways of positively influencing the behavior and social development of individuals with Asperger Syndrome.
Token economy systems	This reinforcer involves the use of items such as chips, play money, and points that are redeemable for a variety of desired items. Token systems are extremely adaptable and offer several advantages for children and youth with Asperger Syndrome: (a) They can be used to support and complement other forms of reinforcement, including contingent activities and social consequences; (b) tokens can be backed up by a variety of reinforcers and are less subject to satiation than other types of reinforcement; (c) tokens can be given without disrupting desired target responses (e.g., a student can be given a chip for appropriate social behavior without interfering with a social activity); (d) tokens allow several individuals with different reinforcement preferences to flexibly use the same program; (e) tokens can be used at almost all times and can be used by professionals, parents, and others; and (f) tokens earned can serve as an empirical basis for evaluating program progress.

Table 4.4
Steps for Developing, Implementing, and Monitoring a Behavior Contract

---

1. Meet with concerned parties.

The student, teacher(s), and parent(s) who will be supporting the contract meet to discuss one target behavior.

2. Determine conditions.

The parties determine when, where, and under what specific conditions the behavior occurs. The contract will be written to address these conditions.

3. Determine who will use the contract and where it will be used.

All persons who will be responsible for contract implementation must know their responsibilities.

4. Determine reinforcement.

Students should be allowed to participate in developing a menu of reinforcers. Reinforcers should be manageable but powerful enough to evoke the desired response. Menus should be rotated often to ensure that student motivation remains high.

5. Determine whether negative consequences will be used.

Contracts are written in a positive way to increase behaviors. Negative reinforcers may not be necessary or even desirable if the positive reinforcers are motivating for the student.

6. Take baseline data.

The parties determine the frequency with which the behavior occurs. Data should be taken over at least 3 to 5 days to ensure that the behavior is typical for the student.

7. Determine reinforcement schedule.

The parties determine how often the student is to receive reinforcers. The contract should be structured so that the student has a successful experience; this will prompt the student to further work toward the contract goals.

8. Determine goals.

The parties determine the criteria for successful completion of the contract. Realistic and reasonable goals should be set, even if those goals do not represent the final level of expectation for the student. When the student consistently reaches the goals, the contract can be modified to target a higher goal.

9. Write the contract.

The contract should be written in terms that specify task and time demands, criteria for accuracy, and available reinforcers.

(continues)

Table 4.4 *Continued.*

---

10. Discuss and sign the contract.

All concerned parties discuss the contract to ensure understanding. It might be necessary to supplement a discussion with drawings or icons for some students with Asperger Syndrome. All concerned parties should receive a copy of the contract.

11. Monitor the contract.

The parties set up a plan to evaluate and modify the contract if needed. All concerned parties should remain in constant contact with each other to ensure that student progress across settings is monitored. If the contract is unsuccessful, the parties need to address task appropriateness, time allotment, and student or environmental factors that could have impeded student progress.

Antecedent Intervention Programs

Antecedent intervention programs may also be designed to successfully manage the behavior of children and youth with Asperger Syndrome. Antecedent modification does not rely on manipulation of consequences. Instead it structures environmental conditions to reduce the probability of a behavior's occurring. For example, a child with Asperger Syndrome who demonstrates her concern over hallway noises by tuning out might best be dealt with by moving her desk away from the source of the noise, as opposed to designing consequences to modify the unwanted behavior. Myriad variables can be used to create favorable antecedent conditions, including curricula and structuring methods.

Behavior-Reduction Strategies

Behavior-reduction strategies involve presenting undesired consequences or withdrawing reinforcement when individuals display specified undesired behaviors. Parents and educators should carefully consider when or whether they will use behavior-reduction approaches with children and youth with Asperger Syndrome. Although these strategies can be effective for some of these children, they are often perceived by students as a form of top-down management and result in additional negative behavior and power struggles.

Behavior-reduction strategies that may be appropriate for children and youth with Asperger Syndrome include differential reinforcement, response cost, and time-out (see Table 4.5).

If behavior-reduction strategies are used, positive alternatives should be implemented first. In addition, the following guidelines should be adhered to:

- Implement behavior-reduction programs through collaborative social contracts that clearly spell out goals, expectations, and consequences.

Table 4.5
Behavior-Reduction Methods

Method	Description
Differential reinforcement	This method attends to and rewards behaviors that are appropriate alternatives or incompatible with an undesired behavior. Thus, unacceptable behaviors are weakened, often by being ignored, while appropriate alternative behaviors are reinforced. Several differential reinforcement options are suitable for use with children and youth with Asperger Syndrome, including reinforcement for engaging less frequently in an undesired behavior, reinforcement for adopting a behavior that is incompatible with the undesired behavior, and reinforcement for engaging in a behavior that is more acceptable than the undesired one. For example, a child who routinely put his hands on the back of a classmate whenever the students were told to "line up" was reinforced for putting his hands in his pockets when standing in line.
Response cost	This method reduces undesired behaviors by removing a reinforcer whenever the undesired behavior is observed. Thus, preferred activities, privileges, free time, and even tokens may be withdrawn when the undesired behavior is displayed. When used in conjunction with reinforcement programs, and when target behaviors are carefully selected to shape desired responses, response cost programs can be effective. For instance, such a program was used in conjunction with a token system and peer-mediated social interaction program to assist a student in remembering not to stroke the faces of peers in her classroom. That is, she was reinforced for standing an appropriate distance from her peers and not touching their faces when talking with them; when she did touch their faces she had a chip removed from her "reinforcement box."
Time-out	This method involves removing an individual from a preferred situation when specified unacceptable behaviors are displayed. Time-out is most effective when (a) it is used with limited numbers of specified unacceptable behaviors (as opposed to being used with a variety of behaviors); (b) when it is for brief periods (typically 2 minutes is adequate time away from ongoing classroom activities); and (c) it is carefully and empirically evaluated for efficacy. For example, a youth with Asperger Syndrome was required to place materials he was using on the floor under his desk and to place his head on his desk without talking or making noises for 2 minutes when he spit in the classroom.

- Apply consequences in a firm, predictable, and direct manner.

- Whenever possible, attempt to implement behavior-reduction programs through self-management and other cognitive-based methods. For example, a child might be trained to quietly lay her head on her desk for 2 minutes when she displays a particular unacceptable behavior.

- Avoid communication and interactions that create opportunities for power struggles and confrontations.

- Be sensitive to conflicts related to behavior-reduction strategies that may escalate into a crisis.

Behavior-reduction strategies should be used only under the following conditions: (a) when positive reinforcement methods have not been successful, or when the nature or severity of a behavior necessitates a more immediate response; (b) if incompatible desired behaviors occur too infrequently (or cannot be sufficiently shaped) to serve as the focus of reinforcement; (c) if an undesired behavior is so intense as to be a danger to an individual; and (d) only when paired with positive reinforcement for desired behavior and systematically, promptly, and consistently carried out in accordance with an approved written plan by well-trained professionals, staff, parents, or a combination. The written plan should include a clear description of specifically what is to be done, who will carry it out, how long the procedures will be continued, and the manner in which the program's success will be evaluated.

Power Struggles

It is common for adults who manage and interact with children and youth with Asperger Syndrome to become entrapped in power struggles, frivolous arguments, and other nonproductive confrontations. For example, one teacher described her frustration in attempting to convince a youth with Asperger Syndrome of the necessity of regular bathing and personal hygiene. In an attempt to convince him of the advantages of good personal hygiene, she said that the youth would be unable to get a good job if he failed to follow accepted hygiene practices. The youth's response was that he intended to pursue a career as a home-based computer programmer. He argued that because he would not be around other people, there was no reason for him to bathe. The teacher then argued that his ability to find a date for the spring dance would be enhanced if he regularly showered and used deodorant. The youth's response to this argument was that he had no interest in attending the school dance but intended to stay home and work on his computer. The teacher reported that this scenario was typical of her interactions with the student. That is, he was highly skilled at entrapping the teacher in power struggles and unproductive arguments that occasionally escalated into major confrontations and crises.

Below are several suggestions for avoiding these common problems.

- Describe in direct terms the behaviors you want the child to display, behaviors about which you are concerned, or both. Inherent in this recommendation is the idea that the child will focus on the behavior of concern rather than on the social consequences of the behavior.

- Avoid suggestive and indirect language. Such language is not only difficult for many children with Asperger Syndrome to understand, it also creates opportunities for power struggles and confrontations. For example, when a student says to a teacher, "I think you are stupid," the teacher should not attribute meaning to the statement by saying, "Why are you upset with me?" The student may not have been upset with the teacher in the first place, but given this lead may pursue it and thereby mask the real intention behind the statement.

- Be sensitive to the fact that children with Asperger Syndrome may appear to lack emotion. Many of these children are unable to understand and show their emotions. Thus, when under stress or when confronted with conflict, these children may appear to be emotionally detached or calm. In these situations, teachers and parents may fail to recognize that the child is experiencing significant stress and emotion that he or she is unable to communicate and overtly manifest. As a result, an interaction may escalate into a bigger problem or even a crisis.

- Apply consistent, firm, and controlled interventions. Adults who interact with children and youth with Asperger Syndrome need to be able to apply firm and predictable directives and consequences. Harsh, punitive, and unexpected directives and consequences often provoke power struggles and increased problems. Moreover, negative and confrontational responses may result in crises.

Concluding Thoughts

As previously noted, effective intervention programs call for designs that support generalization and maintenance. This is especially important for children and youth with Asperger Syndrome, who are well-known for their generalization and maintenance deficits. Self-monitoring and cognitive-based methods based on collaboratively developed social contracts are often most effective in generalizing programs across settings and over time. There is little question that children and youth with Asperger Syndrome present significant social and behavioral challenges for professionals and parents, and therefore require a variety of supports. However, when given appropriate structure, social interaction opportunities, and behavior management support, they can be expected to demonstrate skill and progress.

C H A P T E R

PLANNING FOR LIFE AFTER SCHOOL

All too often information on Asperger Syndrome focuses only on the needs of children. Because Asperger Syndrome is a lifelong exceptionality that can affect an individual's likelihood of enjoying a productive adult life, it is important also to understand how to help these individuals move smoothly into adulthood. Most persons with Asperger Syndrome do not make transitions smoothly without advance preparation. As we have seen in earlier chapters, inherent in Asperger Syndrome are difficulties associated with transitions, changes, and accepting new circumstances.

Transition is an ongoing process that relates to all roles one assumes in life. It includes "life changes, adjustments, and cumulative experiences that occur in the lives of young adults as they move from school environments to more independent living and work environments" (Wehman, 1992, p. 5). Transition of students with disabilities from school to post-school life is a growing concern because of the poor adult outcomes reported in the literature. The need for improved transition-related services is manifested in the high dropout rate and the dismal employment prospects of young adults with exceptionalities.

Students with disabilities need access to a broader array of options at the secondary level that address myriad needs ranging from vocational to social to leisure skills. These needs can be met only through comprehensive programs that reflect the specific strengths of each individual student.

If persons with Asperger Syndrome have received appropriate educational and social strategies and adequate interpersonal support throughout their academic lives, there is no reason to doubt that prognosis for a successful adult life is good. However, these students most often will not easily make the transition from high school to job, vocational school, or college. There must be careful planning to help the person with Asperger Syndrome make appropriate career choices and the transition into adulthood.

In recognition of the needs of youth and young adults with exceptionalities, the federal government has issued mandates regarding planning and providing school programs that address post-school outcomes for students with disabilities. Three pieces of legislation guide transition-related services. The Individuals with Disabilities Education Act (IDEA, 1997) mandates that students participate in their own transition planning meetings. The Americans with Disabilities Act (ADA, 1990) prohibits discrimination against people with disabilities in employment, public accommodations, transportation, and telecommunication. Finally, the Rehabilitation Act Amendments (1992) declare that people with disabilities have the right to self-determination just like their nondisabled peers (see Table 5.1).

Factors That Illustrate the Need for Transition Planning

Those working to prepare students with Asperger Syndrome for adult life should ask themselves, "How can I prepare this student for the world that he or she will be entering?" All too often, schools focus on creating successful students. As a result, young adults with special needs, including those with Asperger Syndrome, experience (a) high dropout rates, (b) high rates of unemployment or underemployment and poor wages, (c) an inability to live independently, (d) unsuccessful attempts at post-secondary training and education, (e) dissatisfaction with their quality of life, and (f) limited opportunities for making personal choices. Instead, education must be focused on the ultimate goal—helping students become successful adults.

High School Dropout Rate

More than 30% of students in secondary special education programs drop out of school. When compared by category of exceptionality, the numbers are more alarming. Although there are not specific numbers for students with Asperger Syndrome, many of these students have been classified as having learning disabilities or behavioral disorders (Frith, 1991; Rutter & Schopler, 1988). The National Longitudinal Transition Study (Wagner, 1989) and Wehman (1992) reported that the dropout rate for students with learning disabilities ranges from 27% to 54%, and the dropout rate

Table 5.1
Legislation That Impacts Transition

Legislation	Description
Individuals with Disabilities Education Act	IDEA (1997) requires that specific outcomes be identified based on student needs, preferences, and interests and that educational programs for all students with disabilities 16 years of age and older "be supported by transition services language that would include instruction, community experiences, development of employment and other post-school adult living objectives, and if appropriate, the acquisition of daily living skills and functional vocational evaluation" (Section 300.18[b]).
	Further, IDEA recognizes a broad definition of transition: "Transition services mean a coordinated set of activities for a student, designed within an outcome-oriented process, which promotes movement from school to post-school activities, including post-secondary education, vocational training, integrated employment, including supported employment, continuing adult education, adult services, independent living or community participation" (Section 300.18[a]).
Americans with Disabilities Act	ADA (1990) offers more choices and options for people with disabilities. It is a form of civil rights legislation, which prohibits discrimination against people with disabilities in employment, public accommodations, transportation, and telecommunications.
Rehabilitation Act Amendments	According to the Rehabilitation Act Amendments (1992), "disability is a natural part of the human experience and in no way diminishes the right of an individual to (a) live independently, (b) enjoy self-determination, (c) make choices, (d) contribute to society, (e) pursue meaningful careers, and (f) enjoy full inclusion and integration in the economic, political, social, cultural, and educational mainstream of American society" (p. 24).

for students with behavioral disorders ranges from 39% to 47%. This high dropout rate implies that secondary special education fails to meet the needs of many students served in these programs.

Unemployment/Underemployment and Poor Wages

According to Wagner (1989), the unemployment rate for young adults with disabilities exceeds 50%. Further, dropouts are generally employed at about one half the rate of graduates. Data regarding employment rates vary from study to study, although persons with learning disabilities have the highest rate of employment. Specifically, employment rates have been set at 70% for persons with learning disabilities (Hardman, Drew, & Egan, 1996). Rumsey, Rapoport, and Sceery (1985) reported on the employment status of 14 adult men (mean age = 28) who had mean verbal intelligence test scores (IQ) of 93. Of these 14 men, 4 were employed in menial jobs, 3 were in sheltered workshops, 4 were in vocational training, 2 were unemployed, and 1 was in a state hospital. Another study (Szatmari, Bartolucci, Bremmer, Bond, & Rich, 1989) reported on 12 men and 4 women who had higher-functioning autism (mean age = 26), with a mean IQ of 92. Seven of this group were employed, 3 were students (all subjects graduated from high school and 7 went on to college), 2 were unemployed, and 4 attended sheltered workshops. Newson, Dawson, and Everard (1982) followed the history of 93 adults with higher-functioning autism who had IQs above 100. They found that 27% were employed competitively; however, 22 of the adults were in sheltered employment and 5 held menial jobs. They also reported that 10 of the individuals were in college and 25 were in some sort of vocational training. Wehman (1992) thus concluded that persons with higher-functioning autism are likely to have poor employment outcomes.

The problem of underemployment is also of concern. The *National Organization on Disability/Harris Survey of Americans with Disabilities* (Harris and Associates, 1994) reported that approximately 70% of all Americans with disabilities were unemployed. Of those who were employed, 75% were employed only part-time. Further, Edgar (1987) reported that although 60% of high-school graduates with disabilities were employed, only 18% earned more than minimum wage. Keel, Mesibov, and Woods (1997), in their study of 100 persons with autism and other developmental disabilities (58% without mental retardation), reported that the individuals were employed an average of 28.6 hours per week with mean earnings of $5.29 per hour. Tantam (1991) synthesized the results of two studies focusing on adults with Asperger Syndrome and found that only 17% were employed. The types of jobs obtained by graduates of special education programs tend to be entry-level jobs with low salaries, few (if any) benefits, and minimal opportunity for advancement (Edgar, 1988; Keel et al., 1997).

Thus, unemployment and underemployment affect persons with Asperger Syndrome, despite their higher than average intelligence. Individuals with higher-functioning autism or Asperger Syndrome who have postsecondary degrees are often unable to obtain or retain jobs at their educational level because of social skills deficits. Although they have abilities that could qualify them for higher paying positions, they end up shelving books at libraries, bagging groceries, washing dishes, or in other low-skill jobs (Donnelly, 1996).

Typically, adults and youth with disabilities are unemployed or underemployed for three basic reasons: (a) lack of interpersonal skills (e.g., work habits, work attitudes, and social communication skills), (b) lack of job-related academic skills, and (c) lack of specific vocational skills to perform more than entry-level personal service jobs (Clark, Carlson, Fisher, Cook, & D'Alonzo, 1991). Individuals with Asperger

Syndrome and higher-functioning autism are unemployed or underemployed primarily because of social skills deficits, sensory issues, problematic behaviors, and poor communication skills (Smith, Belcher, & Juhrs, 1996; Tantam, 1991). Therefore, if students with Asperger Syndrome are to be prepared for the world of work, specific skills must be identified in each of the above areas, and a delivery system must be developed to ensure relevant instruction and services.

Independent Living

According to Wagner (1989), 82% of young adults with disabilities live at home with their parents. Rumsey et al. (1985) reported that of the 14 adults with higher-functioning autism in their study, only 1 lived independently; 3 individuals were in supervised home settings, 1 was in a state hospital, and the remainder (9) lived with their parents. Keel et al. (1997) reported that 58% of the adults with autism and other developmental disabilities that they studied, of which the majority were functioning in the average to above average range, lived at home with parents or caregivers. Only 9% lived in apartments with minimal support. Similarly, Tantam (1991) reported that of 139 adults with Asperger Syndrome, only 8 lived independently. Clearly, based on these data, the goal for independent living for individuals with special needs has not been met by existing programs and services. Therefore, school programs must be designed to address independent living and community survival skills.

Postsecondary Training or Education

Although the number of persons with Asperger Syndrome who attend college is increasing, a 1992 study by Lord and Venter found that only 1 of 18 subjects obtained a university degree (another individual had attended college but left without graduating). Szatmari et al. (1989) found that 7 out of 16 subjects with higher-functioning autism were university graduates. In his report on two studies of the dropout rate of individuals with Asperger Syndrome, Tantam (1991) found that only 11% had any postsecondary education.

Postsecondary school selection is integral to the success of persons with Asperger Syndrome. Often junior colleges or smaller colleges offer the size, structure, and support needed by many who have this exceptionality. Often these institutions have smaller classes, offer more individual support from faculty, and have programs specifically geared to meet the needs of challenged learners. Many colleges and universities provide tutoring and support services. Although the type of service may vary from school to school, it often consists of providing note-takers, test proctors, and auxiliary aides in mainstream classes. Universities often offer basic skills classes, guidance, and counseling.

Individuals with Asperger Syndrome qualify for these services; however, college staff may not have experience or training in providing the unique social supports and time management, organization, and communication skills that would benefit these individuals. For example, one individual with higher-functioning autism had completed the majority of a college course when the professor took him aside to reprimand him for not doing an assigned task. As they discussed the requirement, the professor realized that he had never directly assigned the task but assumed that it was understood. Although the other students followed the professor's implied instructions, the student with higher-functioning autism had understood only those directions that were literal and clearly stated. However, because of his own communication difficulties, the student was unable to defend himself or explain his problem and therefore was penalized (Donnelly & Levy, 1995).

Quality of Life

Quality of life is a relative concept and thus must be considered in terms of each individual. One component of quality of life is that people have the opportunity to make choices (Halpern, 1992). Although employment and the money thus earned play a critical role in quality of life, for most people money does not guarantee satisfaction (Edgar, 1988). Having a social and interpersonal network is also of utmost importance to personal adjustment (Halpern, 1994). It is imperative, therefore, that schools offer specific social skills training to support development of interpersonal skills.

Self-Determination

Self-determination is the ability to make decisions and solve the problems of everyday life. According to Fullerton (1993), self-determination begins with knowing oneself, identifying one's aspirations, and being aware of one's needs. Self-determination makes it possible for the person with Asperger Syndrome to make appropriate choices. The need for this skill is addressed in IDEA (1990) and in the Rehabilitation Act Amendments of 1992. Specifically, IDEA mandates that students participate in their own transition planning meeting. The Rehabilitation Act Amendments declare that people with disabilities have the right to self-determination similar to their nondisabled peers. Individuals with Asperger Syndrome must learn to be more directive in their lives. This can be accomplished by providing them opportunities to make choices and live with the consequences, as well as teaching them to facilitate their own Individualized Education Program (IEP) meetings.

Definition of Transition

In 1994 the Division of Career Development and Transition (DCDT) of the Council for Exceptional Children adopted the following definition of transition:

> Transition refers to a change in status from behaving primarily as a student to assuming emergent adult roles in the community. The roles include employment, participating in post-secondary education, maintaining a home, becoming appropriately involved in the community, and experiencing satisfactory personal and social relationships. The process of enhancing transition involves the participation and coordination of school programs, adult agency services, and natural supports within the community. The foundation for transition should be laid during the elementary and middle school years, guided by the broad concept of career development. Transition planning should begin no later than age 14, and students should be encouraged, to the full extent of their capabilities, to assume a maximum amount of responsibility for such planning. (Halpern, 1994, p. 117)

This definition of transition is the framework for the future of transition planning. That is, along with the mandates of IDEA regarding transition, the DCDT definition provides a structure that is applicable for students with Asperger Syndrome as well as for students with other disabilities. However, effective transition services are not yet in place in many schools throughout the United States. Special educators, therefore, must take a more active and assertive role in including these transition issues in the development of IEPs and program planning they do for their students.

Adjusting to change is difficult for most people, but when a person faces the additional challenge of having Asperger Syndrome, it can be almost overwhelming. IDEA clearly places the initial responsibility for transition planning on the public schools. To be effective, transition planning must occur as a collaborative effort among the student, family, school, rehabilitation counselor, adult service providers, and community members. Together, these partners develop and implement an IEP that provides opportunities for the student with disabilities to acquire the skills necessary to live and work successfully. Identification of post-school outcomes must be the driving force behind the development of long-range goals that will enable students with Asperger Syndrome to achieve their dreams. In this regard, it is important that transition planning involve each individual student and his or her family in making decisions, rather than allowing decisions to be made for the student. The steps of the transition planning process are outlined in Table 5.2.

No single plan is used for all students; a transition plan must be developed for each individual student, addressing specific strengths and concerns. As in other planning, student choice and preferences are key factors in transition planning. The first step toward effective planning involves transition assessment to gain insight into the needs, preferences, interests, and present performance level of a specific student.

Transition Assessment

Because transition is "a lifelong process that begins at birth and relates to all life roles, not just work" (Szymanski, 1994, p. 402), transition assessment must also be a lifelong process that surveys all aspects of one's life.

Table 5.2
Transition Planning Process for Students with Asperger Syndrome

1. Provide student with training to be an active participant in the IEP meeting.

2. Hold IEP meeting to explain transition planning and the roles of the student, parents, and school in the process. Discuss visions for the future. Obtain input regarding assessment, appropriate adult outcomes, types of school programs and services needed, student's vocational interests, and adult service providers to include in IEP process.

3. Review student records. Decide what additional assessment needs to be carried out. Conduct formal and informal assessments. Analyze assessment data. Develop portfolio with student. Assessment will be an ongoing process.

4. Reconvene the IEP team. Discuss assessment results with student and parents. Revisit visions for the future. Plan community experiences, including supervised work experiences. Develop goals and objectives reflecting adult outcomes.

5. Implement the transition IEP and monitor student progress.

6. Reconvene the IEP team annually, or as needed, to modify the IEP.

Independent living skills, personal–social adjustment, and occupational adjustment are the foundations of transition assessment (Clark, 1995). That is, assessment with both formal and informal instruments is the starting point for effective programs. To yield a complete picture of the student, effective assessment determines the student's present level of performance, interests, and preferences. Such information may be collected through reviewing cumulative records, administering and analyzing transition-related measures, interviewing the student, and gathering data from parents, school personnel, rehabilitation counselors, community members, and others who have an interest in helping the student plan for the future.

Formal Assessment

Formal transition assessment includes (a) achievement tests, (b) aptitude tests, (c) adaptive behavior scales, (d) interest inventories (e.g., *Occupational Aptitude Survey and Interest Schedule–Second Edition*, Parker, 1991; *Work Adjustment Inventory*, Gilliam, 1994), (e) adaptive behavior scales (e.g., *Adaptive Behavior Inventory*, Brown & Leigh, 1986), and (f) transition planning instruments (e.g., *The Life Centered Career Education (LCCE) Knowledge Battery*, Brolin, 1992; *The Transition Behavior Scale*, McCarney, 1989; *The Transition Planning Inventory*, Clark & Patton, 1996).

Informal Assessment

Informal assessments provide information from a variety of people who know the student well and who can give their perspectives of the student's capabilities. Informal assessment may specifically address independent living skills, personal–social adjustment, ability to access the community, level of participation in recreation and leisure activities, academic and behavioral issues, dreams for the future, postsecondary training, and educational and vocational interests.

It is most helpful if the student and others are asked similar questions to obtain a complete profile of the student. Hence a variety of methods are used to gather relevant data. For example, informal transition assessment includes (a) personal interviews with the student, parents, teachers, job coaches, and employers; (b) questionnaires and inventories for the student, parents, and teachers (e.g., *The Enderle-Severson Transition Rating Scale*, Enderle & Severson, 1991; *Life Centered Career Education (LCCE) Performance Battery*, Brolin, 1992); (c) self-report checklists for students (e.g., *Self-Directed Search Career Explorer*, Holland & Powell, 1994; *Self-Directed Search–Form R*, Holland, 1994); (d) functional skills rating scales or checklists; and (e) direct observations.

Functional assessment focuses on measuring daily living activities, skills, behavioral performances, environmental conditions, and needs. This type of assessment is conducted in all the environments in which the student functions—home, school, community, and workplace. Such a situational assessment provides, for example, an on-the-job assessment of real work skills and habits or the student's ability to access public transportation.

Person-Centered Transition Planning

Person-centered transition planning focuses on information gathered from the student and significant others in his or her environment. The emphasis is on gaining an in-depth knowledge of the student's skills, interests, and needs through qualitative methods. Person-centered transition planning does not yield a score; however, the information gained through this approach can be helpful in planning career goals for the person with Asperger Syndrome. Two types of person-centered transition planning are *The McGill Action Planning System* (MAPS; Vandercook & York, 1989) and portfolio assessment.

The McGill Action Planning System

Person-center transition planning, such as that offered by MAPS (Vandercook & York, 1989), can assist the person with Asperger Syndrome and those important to him or her to "creatively dream, scheme, plan, and produce results" (p. 205) that lead toward a rich life in a community setting. MAPS asserts that all persons belong in the community and that the basis for community is individual relationships. Relationships are viewed as essential because they are among the most valid markers for measuring quality of life (Vandercook & York), protect individuals from stress, and assist in problem solving.

MAPS is a team approach. That is, the individual with Asperger Syndrome, family members, friends, general and special education personnel, and current employers together develop a strategy for the individual's future. Each of these people should know and care about the individual with Asperger Syndrome; each should also have shared experiences with him or her.

Although the process typically takes about 3 hours, MAPS can occur during one session or be divided among several shorter meetings. All participants are arranged in a half-circle to encourage communication. One person assumes the role of facilitator and guides the meeting. This is typically someone with good listening skills who can encourage team interactions, challenge people to broaden their visions, and keep the group focused on the task at hand. In addition, the facilitator should be comfortable communicating with adults and children from a variety of backgrounds. Planning is optimized when input is gathered equally from all participants. "The importance of each person's contributions should be clearly communicated by the facilitator before the planning begins" (Vandercook & York, 1989, p. 207). The facilitator records ideas generated during the session on chart paper, which becomes a permanent product of the meeting.

During the MAPS session, eight issues are discussed:

1. *What is the individual's history?* To ensure that everyone in the group understands the individual with Asperger Syndrome and others' perspectives, an overview of the individual's history is given. Parents or caretakers and the individual are often in the best position to provide this information. In addition, employers or school personnel can often add relevant information regarding school history, work history, or both.

2. *What is your dream for the individual?* Team members are asked to be forward-thinking—to go beyond the present to identify what the future should hold for the individual, at least for the next 5 years. This is a first step in determining a plan. If group members have a shared vision, they can begin to determine how the dream can be turned into reality. Future dreams should not be fragmented; emphasis should be placed on an integrated future, so dreams should be offered for work, leisure, and personal relationships—all facets of a healthy lifestyle. When the team looks ahead, it can begin to establish specific goals and objectives for an integrated future. The team should address such questions as "Where will the person live?" "What will the dwelling be like and where will it be located?" "Where will the person work?" "What will the work environment be like?" "What community activities will the person engage in?" and "Who will the person spend time with?"

3. *What is your nightmare?* This is typically a difficult issue for those who care about the person with Asperger Syndrome. However, it is important to explore a worst-case scenario. It is only by understanding the nightmare from the perspectives of all involved, including the person with Asperger Syndrome, that it can be prevented. Nightmares could be related to not having friends, living at home with parents as an adult, not having gainful employment, or having limited or no leisure activities to enjoy.

4. *Who is the individual?* Each MAPS participant is asked to describe the person with Asperger Syndrome. Specifically, they are asked, "What words come to mind

when you think of (the person)?" In a round-robin fashion, each person provides a word or phrase; those who have no additional contributions can pass. When the list is complete, key people (family members, long-time acquaintances) are asked to identify three words from the list that best describe the person.

5. *What are the individual's strengths, gifts, abilities, and interests?* Many planning meetings, such as those centered around individual education plans, focus on the student's deficits—the things that he or she cannot do. The MAPS process urges participants to do just the opposite: to identify the positive attributes of the person with Asperger Syndrome. Often this part of the MAPS session begins with a review of the descriptions of the individual (step 4). Following a brief review, the facilitator asks the participants to identify strengths and abilities that will assist the individual in making the transition to the adult world. Identifying interests is an important part of this strategy. Often, commercial interest inventories and transition surveys can be used as a source for this information. MAPS participants often share different perspectives of the individual; thus, it is important that all participants contribute to this question to ensure that the individual is seen as a person with varied interests and abilities.

6. *What are the individual's needs?* During this stage, each participant identifies needs that must be met to help realize the individual's dream. The individual's abilities have previously been identified; needs identification complements that information. Again, each person's unique ideas should be taken into consideration. When the list is complete, needs are prioritized.

7. *What would the individual's ideal day in the community look like and what must be done to make it happen?* MAPS team members plan an ideal day, from the time the person wakes up to the time he or she goes to bed. Planning the day as though the person did not have an exceptionality can often be helpful. After the daily schedule has been planned, the group identifies supports that the individual will need to complete the activities. Then MAPS participants develop a plan to put the supports in place. The plan includes (a) supports needed, (b) actions to take to obtain the supports, (c) person responsible, and (d) timeline. Once these components are identified, the team makes plans to meet again to follow up on progress.

8. *What does MAPS mean to you . . . in a word?* Each team member is given the opportunity to describe MAPS in one word. The team members are asked to share adjectives that are positive or affirming of this process, as well as any concerns they felt about the information generated.

Table 5.3 provides an example of a MAPS session for Dylan, a young man who has Asperger Syndrome.

Portfolio Assessment

For this type of person-centered assessment, a portfolio follows the student throughout school. Portfolio assessment is particularly helpful, as it provides a comprehensive view of the student by consolidating the previously mentioned assessments with additional

Table 5.3
Dylan's MAPS

For Dylan's MAPS process, the team included Dylan, his mother and father (John and Cindy), three 10th-grade friends (Josh, Sam, Brett), his 10th-grade English teacher (Ms. Jones), special education teacher (Mr. Thomas), job coach (Ms. Martin), and Dylan's paraprofessional (Ms. Lines). Dylan's MAPS session took place over 2 days, in sessions of 1½ hours each. Dylan's MAPS process was devised to assist him in taking the correct steps for entering junior college upon completion of his high school education. The first planning session began with introductions.

1. What is Dylan's history?

Dylan's mother, Cindy, identified the members of Dylan's family and shared major events in Dylan's history. When Dylan was approximately 4 years old, his family began to notice that he exhibited unique behaviors. After comparing his development to his older siblings, Dylan's parents took him to a developmental pediatrician and a psychiatrist. Dylan's parents spoke of the apprehension they felt about learning of the results from the medical professionals. At 5 years of age, Dylan was diagnosed with Asperger Syndrome.

Dylan's parents discussed how they have learned to advocate an appropriate education for their son. Both parents feel that he is capable of being successful in school and are encouraging Dylan to look toward entering a junior college after completing high school. With assistance and minimal academic adaptations, Dylan has been able to work on an academic level comparable to that of his age peers.

2. What is your dream for Dylan?

Dylan's parents dream of seeing him live independently with a successful career and hopefully a family in the later future. His parents also dream for Dylan to have a circle of friends who enjoy the same interests. Dylan's friends Josh and Sam hoped that after graduating from college they could work together in a computer company, as they all enjoy working on computers and playing video games. Brett hoped that some day they could travel with their families, just like they had as children. Ms. Jones envisions Dylan's writing science fiction stories upon completing his college education, based on his vivid imagination. Together Ms. Martin and Ms. Lines dream that Dylan will be successful and happy in a career tailored to his personal interests and helping to strengthen his self-esteem. Mr. Thomas dreams that Dylan will lead an independent life, including living on his own and maintaining a job he enjoys. A consistent theme throughout this discussion was Dylan's graduation from college, which would pave the way toward independence and happiness.

3. What is your nightmare?

Dylan's nightmare was that he would not make friends in junior college and would feel uncomfortable, get lost, or both while trying to find all the buildings. Dylan's parents and education team, on the other hand, worried about Dylan's being able to handle the informal structure and independence required for success in junior college, compared to his more structured early education.

(continues)

Table 5.3 *Continued.*

4. Who is Dylan?

Dylan and his MAPS planning team used the following phrases to describe him: He loves to read; he loves to make up stories about aliens; he loves animals; he likes to play video games with his friends; he enjoys helping his father with outside chores; he is interested in writing as a career; he reaches out to his peers; he follows directions while on a job site; he works diligently on paid jobs; he enjoys school; he is working on riding the city bus independently.

5. What are Dylan's individual strengths, gifts, abilities, and interests?

Dylan's strengths, gifts, and abilities include his reading skills, imagination, love of animals, helpfulness, interest in writing, friendliness, ability to follow directions, and interest in developing independent skills.

6. What are Dylan's needs?

Dylan's priority needs were identified by family, friends, and educators.

Family:

- more independence
- larger social circle
- coping strategies when upset and frustrated
- skills necessary to hold down a job without assistance
- classes that prepare him for junior college
- interests that can be studied while attending college
- independent living skills
- happiness

Friends:

- developing and maintaining friendships
- less assistance from teachers
- teachers and peers who understand and try to help him

Educators:

- independent living skills
- independent work skills
- appropriate classes to assist in college coursework
- less dependence on paraprofessional and job coach
- effective and established coping strategies

(continues)

Table 5.3 *Continued*.

- more friends
- self-regulatory skills

7. What would Dylan's ideal day in 10th grade look like and what must be done to make it happen?

Time	Activity
8:25–9:15	study hall (resource room; home base)
9:18–10:05	language arts II
10:08–10:55	geometry
10:58–11:45	biology
11:58–12:35	vocal music/typing
12:35–1:00	lunch
1:03–1:50	P.E./study hall (resource room; home base)
2:00–3:30	community-based programming

To have a successful day, Dylan is placed in full inclusion for his academic classes. Dylan's paraprofessional will be available for assistance, and the general education teachers will make adaptations, with assistance from the special educator, based on Dylan's educational needs. Dylan's study halls will always take place in the resource room, where extra attention can be placed on IEP goals and preparing him for junior college after graduation from high school. Dylan's 10th-grade school year is designed on the same schedule as that of his peers who are also preparing for lifestyle choices after graduation. Academic courses are focused on topics such as food and nutrition, personal health, consumer education, job skills, and computers. These courses provide students with an appropriate background that facilitates independence and assists in the transition to a less stressful college experience.

Dylan participates in many extracurricular activities. These activities include building theater sets for fall plays and spring musicals and participating in Large Group Speech through choral reading. Dylan has been attending open gym on Sundays at the high school, where his peers play basketball and socialize. He also assists in managing a sports team each season: football in the fall, and basketball in the winter. He keeps statistics for the baseball team in the summer. In addition, he throws the discus for the track team.

8. MAPS . . . In a word

The last request of the facilitator was for everyone to describe in a word what he or she thought of the MAPS process. The following descriptors were generated: interesting, teamwork, exhausting, powerful, continuous, integrated, whole, empowering, functional, and directive. Overall, the MAPS process was viewed positively by Dylan and his family, friends, and educators. It is believed to be a starting point to a successful college career for Dylan.

[*Contributed by Katherine Tapscott*]

student information. The student is integral to portfolio planning; he or she helps decide what information is included in the portfolio. A portfolio may include (a) summaries of formal, informal, and functional assessments; (b) summaries of transition planning assessments; (c) videos of actual job performance; (d) interviews with employers and co-workers, friends, and family; (e) videos of participation in recreational and leisure activities; (f) videos of daily living and functional living skills performances; and (g) letters of reference from friends, school personnel, roommates, employers, and co-workers. As the person gains new skills, the career portfolio can be updated similar to a resume or vita (Bernhardt, Cole, & Ryan, 1993; Sarkees-Wircenski & Wircenski, 1994).

Portfolio transition assessment is ideal for students with Asperger Syndrome because it is an ongoing process that illustrates the growth, change, and abilities of the student. As the student matures, areas of strengths and concerns will change, as will areas of interest. Therefore, transition-related areas must be continually assessed and reassessed to plan and develop appropriate IEPs and to modify programs to meet changing needs. The importance of transition assessment cannot be overstated. It is the cornerstone of effective transition planning.

Life-Span Approach to Transition Planning

Transition is a lifelong process that emphasizes the whole person across his or her many environments (Clark et al., 1991; Repetto & Correa, 1996). The life-span approach to transition is based on the premise that transition is not a product, but an ongoing process (Szymanski, 1994), with career interests and aspirations evolving over time. To encourage transition across the life span, students with Asperger Syndrome need to participate in age-appropriate activities with age peers (students with and without disabilities). These students also need to be contributing members of the community, participating in activities that are of interest to them. In this context, community or school mentors who share interests with these students can help them develop their interests into employable skills. Schools should help facilitate relationships with mentors and friendships that will grow into a support network. In addition, schools must provide a comprehensive program that includes academic support and community-based education focusing on employment, independent living, social skills, and life skills.

Academic Support

Persons with Asperger Syndrome need opportunities to interact in work and leisure activities with nondisabled peers and to have age-appropriate responsibilities. During the preschool years, typical students begin to develop awareness of roles and responsibilities by observing others at work and by playing. Students with Asperger Syndrome may not be aware of others or participate in typical play that imitates adult work behavior. Therefore, teachers may need to draw these children's attention to adults and children engaging in domestic and professional work in their environment.

Peer social groups can assist students with Asperger Syndrome in learning and rehearsing appropriate skills. For example, in elementary and junior high school, students with Asperger Syndrome should be taught good work habits and interpersonal skills while they increase their social skills and career awareness. In later school years, areas of special interest can be broadened and molded into employable skills while the ability to live independently is acquired. Program planning and goals need to be flexible to meet the changing abilities and needs of the student with Asperger Syndrome.

Career Planning and Community-Based Instruction

One of the first steps in community-based instruction is to help students become aware of the many types of vocational options that are available. Often persons with Asperger Syndrome have a narrow range of interests and as a result, have little or no idea of the wide variety of employment opportunities that exist. Following the development of awareness, community-based instruction includes matching student interests and skills to jobs. It is important to understand that in most cases, persons with Asperger Syndrome have unlimited career options and great potential for success if they receive opportunities that match their skill levels, interests, and needs. Students with Asperger Syndrome who like to work outdoors could hold positions such as gardener, surveyor, or landscaper, depending on their other interests and skills. Those who prefer to work in solitude may be best suited for positions that allow for minimal interaction, such as a computer programmer or accountant. Community-based instruction gives students with Asperger Syndrome opportunities to try various jobs and to practice the skills they have learned in school.

Students must realize their potential and be encouraged to work to attain their goals. Finding success in community work experiences, for example, may encourage some students to seek further training or education after high school. Whatever course a student decides to pursue after high school will be smoother if the foundation has been established during school.

Paid Work Experience

Paid work experience under the direction of educators enables students to work during school hours and to maintain employment after graduation. This arrangement not only provides a monetary incentive, but also enables the student to experiment with a variety of occupations.

Because many individuals with Asperger Syndrome have difficulty understanding the importance of learning through simulation and thus often refuse to participate in such activities, opportunities to participate in a "place-train" model of supported employment is often more successful. The place-train model teaches essential work behavior in the natural setting—the actual job. Rather than waiting until the student has learned the required behaviors in a setting that is unmotivating, students can learn needed skills where they will be used—on the job site (Wehman & Moon, 1988).

Community work experiences allow the student to experience firsthand what different jobs entail and to develop friendships within the community. The opportunity to develop relationships also allows students with Asperger Syndrome to become an integral part of their community. For example, as students participate in community experiences, their neighbors get to know them on a personal level, which hopefully will lead to further acceptance of individual differences.

Functional Curriculum Approach

A functional curriculum approach should be a part of the student's school day. For example, students with Asperger Syndrome who are learning functional skills could learn to plan a budget, use a checking account, complete applications, and follow deadlines for turning in work. They could also be taught much-needed community-based pragmatic skills: how to speak to an employer, how to ask for a day off, how to negotiate for a raise, and how to initiate and maintain peer interactions. These skills are essential for persons with Asperger Syndrome, whether they plan on entering an institution of higher education, a vocational training school, or a workplace following high school.

Developing the Transition-Related IEP

After careful analysis of the transition assessment results and the collaborative efforts of the student, family, school personnel, rehabilitation counselor, adult service providers, and interested community members, it is time to develop the IEP to ensure that the school will provide the programs and services to meet the needs of this individual student. This process is quite similar for all students, regardless of the student's age or level of disability.

Concluding Thoughts

Historically, students with Asperger Syndrome and other developmental disabilities have not fared well in adult life. They are often underemployed or unemployed and frequently are not provided opportunities to live independently. Transition planning based on a variety of informal, formal, and person-centered measures can help persons with Asperger Syndrome and their families plan for a successful and productive life. The life-span approach to transition will help students with Asperger Syndrome move from school to post-school life, maximizing their options for employment, living, and recreation.

UNDERSTANDING ASPERGER SYNDROME AND ITS IMPACT ON THE FAMILY

Parents and families of individuals with Asperger Syndrome contend with a variety of challenges for which they have little or no training. As with parents and families of individuals with any disability, they experience anger, disappointment, frustration, and a variety of other emotions related directly or indirectly to the disorder. At the same time, however, they are expected to understand and support their family member with Asperger Syndrome without the benefit of widespread information about and understanding of the condition. Hence, in addition to having to deal with significant personal challenges with little or no support, these families often must educate others about the mysteries, characteristics, and challenges associated with Asperger Syndrome.

It is for these reasons that we have included in this book the voices and reflections of parents and family members of individuals with Asperger Syndrome. Our hope, and the hope of those who have contributed to this chapter, is that their experiences will benefit other parents and families as well as professionals who work with individuals with Asperger Syndrome.

Case Examples

 ## MICHELLE

Michelle is a teenager with Asperger Syndrome. Her diagnosis was made when she was 12 years old. Before then, Michelle's odd, stubborn, detached nature was a mystery, as were the means to help her.

Michelle was always a "difficult" child, whose dogged adherence to her own unique way of doing things has made life difficult for her and those around her. Even her birth was difficult and unique, in that she was delivered face up (the reverse of the norm). This might have been endearing, but as with so much of Michelle's subsequent "uniqueness," the effect was unnecessary travail. In this case, face up meant 23 hours of painful labor for Mom.

Michelle was not an easy infant to love. She showed displeasure regularly and effectively by uncontrolled, unrelenting screaming. This was especially so on occasions marked by change. A car trip at 3 months, for example, meant ceaseless wailing on the road. The only peace came with sleep, and that was unpredictable and scarce. Hotel rooms, relatives' homes—any strange environment was met in a similar way. Eventually, Mom and Dad resigned themselves to the idea that this was just "colic," even though it didn't always fit what the book said, especially the part about "gone in 3 months" (6 or 8 were more like it!).

As an infant, Michelle was always a bit stiff and squirmy when held. She never cuddled, and she resisted physical closeness and affection. Although she could be engaged socially in play, and enjoyed silliness, she was not inclined to interact with others, and preferred playing by herself. Near the end of the first year she began to demonstrate a far-away look when in the company of other children. A photo of her first birthday party is typical—four other little girls all focused on some minor event, while Michelle has a trance-like expression, her thoughts focused elsewhere. Then, as now, Michelle was rarely "in the moment." She is barely aware of people, objects, events happening now. Her mind is elsewhere—actively thinking—but not here, not now.

Socially, Michelle the toddler was much the same. Her mom made repeated efforts to foster friendships by inviting little girls to play, but things seldom "clicked." Usually, Michelle seemed disinterested. Even when Michelle tried to interact with others, her efforts were awkward and ineffective.

At about this same time, though, Michelle did find a friend, a neighbor girl named Tamika. Tamika was quite slow, and almost as unique in her behavior as Michelle (e.g., Tamika, who was supremely self-assured, unself-consciously kept a pacifier in her mouth most of the time, well into her 5th year!).

The two girls were almost constant companions from the age of 1 until 6 years, when Tamika and her family moved. Each seemed oblivious to the oddities in the other. And although their personalities did not "mesh," they succeeded as friends by adopting a "parallel" style of play, each doing her own thing, but "together." This style persisted until Tamika moved, well past the age when parallel play is considered "normal."

At age 2, Michelle got a baby brother. While Brother assumed secondary importance to friend Tamika, he was nonetheless a close companion, whose acceptance of Michelle was total. Michelle, for her part, took a protective role toward her baby brother.

At age 4, Michelle was enrolled in preschool 3 days per week. Her parents, convinced that she was very bright, were shocked at the negative reports from her teachers. They were concerned that Michelle did not interact well with the other children—very concerned. About the same time, Michelle developed an odd attachment to a tree by the house. An old scrub oak in the back yard inexplicably became "her" tree, a fond attachment which was mentioned several times a year, and lasted almost a decade. Her affection was demonstrated by long periods spent at the base of the tree and by excited, animated remarks about the tree, Michelle's "old friend."

Grade school was an interesting time. Standard IQ testing conducted with all of the kindergarten students indicated that Michelle had a full-scale IQ of 130. Nevertheless, her teacher, an older woman with a definite authoritarian bent, was unhappy with Michelle's work and behavior. She seldom made appreciative remarks about Michelle to her parents. Instead she often seemed disgusted with Michelle, and Michelle often appeared sad and frustrated. Not surprisingly, the teacher recommended that Michelle repeat kindergarten.

Happily, the second time around, Michelle got a new and very different kindergarten teacher. Teacher number 2 obviously liked Michelle, and had an appreciation for her unique ways. This teacher, in fact, appeared to like all children, seemed happy and secure about herself, and was not hung up on authority. This was a perfect recipe for Michelle, and it produced a happier, more content student. Over the years, this teacher model worked well for Michelle on many occasions. Contrariwise, stern, authoritarian teachers, while beneficial for many students, were bad for Michelle. Michelle was never able to please the regimentarian, whose emphasis on order and punctuality was largely beyond Michelle's grasp. Teachers like this could be counted on to have a bad effect both on her performance and on her behavior, and especially on how she felt about herself.

Happily, the ensuing 4 years of school saw a succession of reasonably accepting, supportive teachers who allowed Michelle to be herself. They usually found her interesting and engaging, in her own unique way. They were realistic about her progress, but nonetheless were careful not to be overly critical of her spotty schoolwork and inattentiveness in class. And although Michelle was by no means an ideal student, she was compliant and never disruptive.

Michelle's behavior around other children continued to be unusual in grade school. Described as aloof, unattached, and a lone wolf, Michelle rarely interacted with other kids at school, unless as part of a group game directed by the teacher. During free times in recess, Michelle would typically wander about by herself, happily engrossed in her own thoughts. The main exception to this pattern, and it happened regularly, was that she would often seek out adults for "conversation." The conversation was usually one-sided, with Michelle rambling on in a somewhat pedantic fashion about some topic of her choosing. Out of politeness and a certain degree of interest, teachers allowed this, but would eventually break it off to discourage monopolizing by Michelle and to encourage her to mix with other kids.

Home life for Michelle during most of grade school followed the pattern set earlier. Friendship with Tamika remained the same as before, until Tamika moved. And despite the central and important role that Tamika had played, her parting, although duly noted on many occasions, was not met with any overt sadness or sense of loss. Attempts to foster interaction with "normal" girls continued to be unsuccessful, but were seemingly more painful for Michelle's parents than for Michelle.

A move to a different neighborhood around age 8 brought a new selection of potential playmates for Michelle, but no improvement. One interesting relationship did develop out of the move, however. Michelle came to revere a pretty and rather snobbish little girl next door and made overtures of friendship. A relationship did develop, due to Michelle's obvious high regard for the neighbor and the neighbor's esteem for anyone who recognized how wonderful she was. After several months, however, the relationship grew tiresome for the neighbor, who abruptly ended it.

Michelle, unfazed and unashamed, made repeated, earnest, though awkward efforts to regain the friend. After several failures, she hit on something that worked—she became the neighbor's servant, performing all sorts of tasks in return for the attentions of the "friend." Even when this unusual arrangement lost its appeal for the neighbor, Michelle accepted this second loss of the friend without remorse or humiliation. Unfortunately, this detached attitude toward social acceptance was not to last forever.

At home, the grade schooler Michelle spent a great deal of her time alone in her room. Although there was a brief interest in stamp collecting, most of her activities seemed pointless. She had difficulty maintaining attention to any particular activity, and thus would rapidly pass from one activity to another, never completing anything. Dad made a fairly regular habit of reading to Michelle in her room, especially *Highlights* magazine, which gave mutual delight. Michelle liked doing homework with Dad at this stage, especially when Dad presented the material verbally. It was also at this stage that Michelle's extreme inherent messiness became apparent in her room, at the table, and particularly at school, where her disorganization was always duly noted by the teacher.

Michelle obviously did not want to be messy and disorganized, and she was never hostile at attempts from others to help her "shape up." She simply was incapable of sustaining organization. It is likely that her inattention to the "here and now" made neatness seem unimportant. Organization may also have demanded too dear a price, requiring as it does a sustained marshaling of attention that for Michelle was very tedious, tiring, and even exhausting.

Grade 5 marked a significant change at school. Not only did the difficulty of the work increase at this time, but the teacher departed from his predecessors' laissez-faire attitude. Instead, he demanded conformity in schoolwork and was unwilling to be flexible about this. Despite her native intelligence, Michelle was generally unable to cope with the demands of finishing work and turning it in of her own accord, not to mention keeping track of homework assignments, etc. Efforts on the part of her parents to modify teacher demands in light of Michelle's shortcomings were not successful. It was the teacher's belief that developing organizational ability and responsibility came first. Any child could do it, if he or she would only will it. This remained the predominant refrain of Michelle's teachers for the next 4 years, the end result being that Michelle did not improve noticeably in responsibility or organization; besides, she of course learned very little.

The rigidity of the fifth-grade teacher was repeated by the sixth-grade teacher, only much more so. Although dynamic and effective with most of her class, this teacher was unable to accept nonconformity in a student, or messiness, or disorganization, or any of the many traits that flow out of these three. This teacher could make the trains run on time, but she was unconcerned about those who were left at the station, usually Michelle. In fact, Michelle's nonconformity eventually made the teacher dislike her.

At the same time that Michelle's teachers were becoming convinced of her unworthiness, Michelle was reaching the same conclusion on her own. As an early adolescent, Michelle was experiencing the same growth of self-awareness that most kids do. And while for most kids this process is positive, in Michelle's case it was not. Up until now, the fact that Michelle was a loner who was unable to "connect" with other children and be part of the group had been of little concern to her. She was content to spend recess and lunch virtually alone and was unconcerned about her lack of friends.

However, once self-awareness developed, Michelle's realization that she did not fit in was very painful. As a result, she became depressed, and her cheerful demeanor changed to one of sadness, frustration, and even anger. At home, she stayed in her room almost exclusively. In order to relieve stress, she began the distressing habit of cutting on herself with a pin or small knife.

The cuts were superficial and not dangerous. But they were obvious enough to send shock waves throughout the school and family. Although it was clear to those who knew her well that the cutting was not intended to produce harm, but to relieve stress, "caring" adults at school and elsewhere were anxious about it. Questions about suicide naturally followed. "Yes," she sometimes thought about dying. "Yes," she had thought about suicide. As you might imagine, this was all it took to unleash a flood of attention. Michelle, who was suffering from an inability to connect and to engage others in conversation, had found a means to be important, to avoid being ignored.

What followed was not good! Not only did Michelle receive endless attention by adults and kids alike for disquieting remarks, she quickly learned the game and became very good at it. Manipulation did not enter into it, though. To Michelle she was simply getting what she needed in the best way she knew how. Of course, any child could be seduced by this sort of instant attention. But while most early adolescents sense the cost and avoid it entirely, or else give it up fairly rapidly, Michelle did not understand, and so she persisted. And once this suicide material lost its impact, it was replaced with other shocking things. Sadly, Michelle could not comprehend the negative impact it was having on peers, for whom the sense of her oddness and undesirability was only strengthened.

This eventually led to the psychologist's office, where the downward spiral continued. In an effort to uncover any underlying psychopathology, the psychologist encouraged Michelle to express any morbid or horrible thoughts that might be lurking in the dark recesses of her mind. Michelle, for her part, was most willing to oblige. In time she produced loads of shocking fantasies for the doctor who, in exchange, provided Michelle with lots of high-quality, satisfying attention.

Both doctor and patient were duped. For the psychologist, the result was a wildly mistaken diagnosis of extremely morbid personality where none existed, based on musings of a patient whose need for attention was fulfilled by inventing shocking things to say. For Michelle, it merely reinforced the notion that shocking remarks work! Unhappily, following the lesson of the psychologist, remarks about cutting and suicide became even more common, supplanted in time by fictitious musings about her lesbianism, multiple personalities, and criminal friends.

 BRENT

Santa Claus was preparing to visit the preschool our son attended. It was time to question the children singly about Christmas presents they hoped to get. Suddenly our boy pulled

Santa's chair away, and jolly old St. Nick went down in a heap. The other children and their parents didn't know what to make of it. Neither did my wife or I.

More than 8 years were to pass before we received a diagnosis of Asperger Syndrome, often called high-functioning autism. The diagnosis would at least place in clearer focus the preschool embarrassment and over a dozen other examples of our son's quirkiness.

While Santa has reportedly recovered, Mom and Dad are worn slick dealing with pediatricians, psychiatrists, psychologists, allergists, pharmacologists, therapists, educational consultants, and counselors—not to leave out medical insurers, public and private school personnel, and home schoolers. Oh, yes—we also moved 900 miles to a presumably allergy-friendly environment (where new allergies replaced old ones) and within a couple of months moved right back to accommodate homesickness. We were prepared to go to any length.

The Asperger diagnosis, however late, now helps lessen what must be called "parental panic." We're sharper about what to expect, about how we should deal with it, about being ready to cope with the unexpected.

One might reasonably ask whether such a diagnosis also brings apprehensions about our son's future—about his prospects for navigating successfully the maze of social rituals, the most stressful of all dark places Asperger's people must enter. Yes, the diagnosis has brought new worries, particularly about his impending adolescent dating and whether he will understand fully the commitment required for marriage, for child-rearing, for productive work relationships. There's also the worry about which Asperger's traits he might pass to his children.

And yet—with all the day-to-day adjustments for us as well as those future uncertainties—there's an unexpected "up" side. More on that in a moment.

The Asperger Syndrome diagnosis and our subsequent examination of the literature has helped us understand much that has haunted us for years, questions such as:

- Why, when he was a toddler and able to speak clearly, did our son respond with only a vacant stare to our cheery greetings?

- Why did he resist hugs, yet during naps with Mom or Dad seemed to glue the full length of his body to our backs?

- Why did he throw himself to the floor and scream when anyone turned on a vacuum cleaner?

- Why were his questions becoming more and more repetitious, as though he'd never heard our answers?

- Why, through most of his boyhood, couldn't our son catch a ball one-to-one with Dad or learn to throw it accurately?

- When a classmate's dog died and our son learned of it, why did our boy react by laughing in the bereaved youngster's face?

- Why after play experiences that brought resentful howls from teammates did our son insist that he'd only wished to help the other side?

- Why in his earlier school years did he become terribly disoriented when having to shift to new tasks?

- Where did all those on-again, off-again tics come from—odd hand and arm movements, incessant coughing, stuttering, loud nose blowing?

- What triggers those periodic and frightening anxiety attacks, at times marked by vigorous self-biting and hand banging?

- Why do "friends" abandon him with such heartbreaking consistency?

- Why for so long was he uncomfortable in pants snug at the waist and intent on wearing inappropriate but softer sweat clothes?

- When our son is being introduced to individuals, why does his body stiffen and his face assume a startled expression—even though he can address a roomful of people with relative ease?

- How is it possible for him to play the piano with near perfection for an audience when the performance follows unsteady practice sessions that frequently end in emotional breakdowns?

- Why are his reading comprehension scores declining alarmingly?

- When furnished with a wide range of reading material at an early age, why did he immerse himself instead in promotional books from automobile showrooms?

- What accounts for the near-zero motivation and low energy level in a youngster of such high intelligence?

- What makes our son convert a simple apology into a kind of persevering self-flagellation—to a point that used to drive Mom and Dad to distraction?

Where there were only guesses before there are now answers—though of limited satisfaction—to all these questions in the context of Asperger Syndrome. Notice also from the varying tenses that there's been a movement forward in our son's ability to shift tasks, catch a ball, dress more appropriately. There's also been progress in terms of his parents' enlarged capacity for patient understanding and growing conviction that some Asperger's traits can be short-circuited, if not overcome.

Though doctors can judge where the combinations of behavior might place a child on the continuum of autism, they're far from knowing why Asperger children manifest these behaviors. And there is little consensus on whether the most distressing Asperger symptoms can truly be changed, whether by behavior modification or through biochemistry.

We parents, on whom medical practitioners depend for answers to a greater extent than we might have expected, are pretty much at the same stage as those who first tried to invent the wheel. Parents must first examine every clue to what might benefit or in some way comfort their children, try it, try it again, and failing in that approach, back off and try something else.

For example, my 12-year-old son and I attended a conference of the organization More Advanced Autistic People (MAAP). Among the many things I learned was that Asperger children like to be "wrapped" or "cocooned" at times (which helped explain his early-childhood napping position). My son had for months before the conference developed a nightly habit of coughing and twitching 30 to 90 minutes before falling asleep. When he asked (in the motel room on the way back from the conference) whether he could lie down with me, I said "Sure!" and proceeded to stroke his head slowly, rhythmically, and very gently. He coughed maybe eight or ten times and fell asleep within 5 minutes. On subsequent tries of this same method at home I got it down to less than 2 minutes. At this writing such stroking doesn't seem necessary at all, though we might expect that tic to return. The lesson? He may be growing up and almost as tall as Dad, but there's still a little boy in there—my little boy with special needs.

Those needs now oblige us to know the effects of loud noises on our son and to do everything to avoid them. (Remember the vacuum cleaner?) For instance, unproductive yelling at our younger son, who vexingly has Attention-Deficit/Hyperactivity Disorder, has been cut way down. Our Asperger's boy's sensory problems also involve touch and the way in which various articles of clothing affect or discomfort him.

Conversations and social experiences are being given new attention so that Mom and Dad might discover how to clear the path through what is a terrifying jungle for people with Asperger Syndrome. We now know more about the way our older boy thinks and about the neurologically based differences between how he sees the world and how we do.

We've discovered a few Asperger's traits in ourselves, which has helped explain past and present quirks to ourselves and each other. It's given us clues as to how we may help our boy outgrow similar traits that we know served us poorly.

We still find it hard to believe it took so many professionals so many years of sifting through our son's symptoms before two working in concert came up with Asperger Syndrome.

Had we known sooner what we know now, we could have averted a number of school crises that have begun to grow more severe in recent years, particularly the way our son's addressing or questioning teachers is customarily perceived by them. He's flippant with teachers—because he has a sense of humor that doesn't take social conventions into account. He may be saying to himself, "I'll try this and see what happens." And when teachers hand out assignments involving six or seven steps and deadlines far in the future, such as a term paper or research project, our boy is overwhelmed. As a sign of wanting to do the right thing about such assignments, he may particularize point by point in order to understand everything expected of him. But it's that questioning that drives teachers up the wall. Seeing that reaction, he decides to run from the task mentally and emotionally. The night before the assignment is due he may or may not tell Mom or Dad about it and seek help.

Because the label of high-functioning autism now places our son as a public school student under the protection of the Americans with Disabilities Act, that law is being applied helpfully now. Unlike the experiences of the past, not all teachers are dismissing our boy's quirks by saying things like, "I know when he's pulling my chain." Thanks to the in-house presence of middle-school special education professionals, something resembling a coping network is now on alert. We're not saying there's intervention before a crisis such as an anxiety attack. But there is certainly new school staff energy being applied to emergencies involving our son so that those situations don't get worse. We've even noticed a growing preference by the special staff to "work through" the problem at school rather than sending him home. We'd always given him that alternative to ensure he knows there's a safe haven, but maybe their way will be better for him.

Because Asperger's children tend to be couch potatoes, given their difficulties in sports, our son was becoming obese. My wife came up with the idea of hiring a personal trainer, who now visits frequently to work out with the boy. Within a very short time our son started looking better. He seemed also to be feeling better, physically and emotionally. We don't care what this may cost if it works to make our boy healthier and happier.

Earlier I indicated an "up" side to our sudden immersion in the world of Asperger Syndrome and to our learning that our son has this now identifiable, though complicated, disability. We draw optimism from such positives as his abilities in art, music, computers, math, and in memorization, analysis, and special reasoning skills. Where will they lead him? In her book, Thinking in Pictures, Temple Grandin (whom we heard speak at the MAAP conference) makes a good case for the possibility that Albert Einstein may have had what we now call Asperger Syndrome. She names other notables with these traits. Dr. Grandin has high-functioning autism and is a remarkable achiever in animal science. She has designed one third of all livestock-handling facilities currently used in the United States. Just knowing that such a productive life as hers is possible has brightened the outlook for our Asperger's child.

As parents we're now beyond "Why us?" And because Asperger's children show nearly as many differences from one another in symptoms as they do similarities, support group help is limited. Our main focus now is to guide him toward doing his best in every way, while he's still at an age when we can be of maximum influence.

Whenever we look at or listen to this beautiful, talented, heart-of-gold youngster and realize we're lucky enough to be able to say "He ours!" we have no doubt about our abilities to meet whatever challenges Asperger Syndrome presents.

 EDWARD

Living with a child with Asperger Syndrome means truly living life one day at a time—frequently 1 minute at a time. Even when the correct diagnosis has finally been reached and you begin to understand where your child's problems come from, living with Asperger Syndrome causes a tremendous amount of frustration and stress for everyone in the family. It affects every aspect of our lives and at times threatens to overwhelm us. But this is our son, so we continue to struggle to make it through one more day.

Each day we are on guard because we never know what situation we may have to deal with. It might be just one of the many misunderstandings that occur so often when Edward is with other people in which we need to intervene to mediate, interpret, or guide him through. It is just as likely that we may have to deal with a situation that is potentially dangerous to himself or others because he doesn't understand cause and effect. As he has gotten older, his drastically inappropriate behaviors that occur when he is overstressed have become less frequent but more dangerous. Since there are no warnings to let us know that Edward is becoming stressed, and he is unable to recognize this himself, we all live with at least a slight "fight or flight" response whenever he's around. We must be prepared to take quick, decisive action in situations we would never even have thought of having to deal with. Even though we know that his aggressive and dangerous actions are a stress reaction and not usually related to what is currently going on around him, or aimed at "the victim" personally, it is impossible not to get upset when they occur.

After trying many different medications with only moderate improvement, we have come to the conclusion that the best way to help our son is to decrease his stress level. At home we have done this by taking him off the family chore chart and giving him only one task at a time. We make sure he has "quiet" time in his room at frequent intervals throughout the day and carefully supervise him at all times. Probably the two most important ways we try to decrease his stress at home are to prevent circumstances and situations that are likely to get Edward into trouble and to maintain a strict routine (which frequently means lots of reminding and refocusing of his attention to the task at hand).

Unfortunately, we have not been able to get adequate accommodations outside of home. Since Edward, now in high school, gets good grades when he does the work and doesn't act or look like an obviously handicapped person, there is a refusal to accept the fact that he is handicapped. They choose not to understand that in spite of his high intelligence, his comprehension of basic life skills, such as right and wrong, self-responsibility, cause and effect, and social obligation and expectations, is similar to that of a low-functioning autistic child. His ability to perceive, interpret, and respond to other people's cues is also deficient. Since he is unable to filter stimuli, he often withdraws into himself or behaves inappropriately when he's overwhelmed, the same way an autistic child does. They choose not to see that because of these short circuits he will not learn appropriate attitudes and behaviors simply by being around "normal" peers. It's easier for them to think that Edward is intentionally behaving this way or that he's just "odd" and that his inappropriate behavior should simply be ignored.

The result of this "head in the sand" attitude about Edward's handicap on the part of the educational system is that we have been forced to watch him struggle on a daily basis with situation after situation that confuses, frustrates, and angers him because he doesn't understand what's going on or the need to do what's expected of him. Because he can't recognize his feelings, he has no way to deal with them, so his stress level builds, causing more and more inappropriate and aggressive behavior. Since all his energy is spent just trying to get through the day at school, he frequently arrives home exhausted and ready to explode from all the stresses and confusions of the day, and the family bears the brunt of it.

In an attempt to try to help him relieve some of this stress, Edward and I have a talk immediately after school each day. We talk about things that are on his mind, good and bad. I try to explain to him why situations went the way they did and to help him put things in perspective. We also use this time for coaching on situations that are likely to occur in the near future, in hopes that this will help him to deal a little better with them and decrease some of his anxiety.

Unfortunately, this doesn't always work, especially if he is angry, stressed, or upset. We have tried to teach him appropriate ways to cope with his feelings, but since he isn't able to recognize what he is feeling, he isn't able to use alternatives when needed. If we encourage him to use them, he becomes very belligerent and angry because he views it as making him do something else he doesn't see a need to do. This only adds to the problem. As Edward becomes more and more stressed, we see a definite increase in random aggression toward his younger brother and sister and, more recently, myself. The aggression takes the form of instigation of activities that are likely to cause the smaller person to get hurt, unnecessary verbal attacks, or physical actions that they can't protect themselves against because he's so much bigger than they are. Even though we have him spending more quiet time in his room at these times, the stress continues to build, and eventually Edward begins to hear voices. He begins to do things that are irrational and potentially dangerous such as stealing, running away, mixing chemicals or body waste products into drinking or grooming products, experimenting with fire, and many other things most of us would never even think of, much less act on.

Naturally, Edward's problems also affect his younger siblings, Nathaniel and Rosa. It is difficult for them to understand why the big brother they love will suddenly and without apparent cause do or say something that hurts or upsets them. Although most of the time Edward's behaviors are merely annoying or years below his age level, the unpredictability of his behavior has caused his younger siblings to be very wary around him. As Nathaniel, now 8 put it, "I wish I knew if Edward was going to act like my big brother or my little brother so I'd know how to act around him. I can't trust him."

It also puzzles them when Edward continues to repeat inappropriate behaviors that they have long since learned are wrong. Even Rosa, at the young age of 5, recognizes that many of Edward's behaviors and attitudes are "little kid." Since our younger children can't begin to comprehend how someone can quote rules word for word, yet not be able to apply them to himself, we have had to come up with other ways to help them keep their balance of right and wrong. We do things like giving Edward exactly the same consequence for breaking a rule as we do the other two. If the consequence for Nathaniel and Rosa is to stand in the corner for 2 minutes for breaking a certain rule, when Edward breaks that rule, he stands in the corner for 2 minutes. While we older and hopefully wiser folks know that since Edward doesn't connect the consequences with his actions, he is not learning from the situation, we are setting a pattern of consistency for our younger children by letting them know that wrong is wrong no matter who did it, and that the consequence will be the same. It also reassures them to know that Edward's inappropriate actions toward them will be addressed. His handicap is not an excuse for bad behavior.

Another problem area, especially for Nathaniel, is playing with friends. Since Edward's friendships do not continue outside the school setting, he tends to intrude into whatever activity Nathaniel and his friends are doing and to monopolize the situation. The frequent outcome is that Nathaniel winds up getting excluded altogether, which of course makes him angry. The best way we've found to protect Nathaniel's right to have his own friends is to divert Edward into another activity away from the younger kids unless one of us is able to be close by to step in as needed.

Probably the most frequent area of frustration for both siblings is Edward's preference to sit and do nothing or to "zone" (enter the "safety zone") of television or the computer to the exclusion of all else. They enjoy doing things with other people and can't understand that Edward is much more comfortable when he's not interacting with others. After several unsuccessful attempts to get Edward to play with them, they tend to take it personally even though it's not meant that way. Sometimes we allow Edward some "zone" time. Sometimes Mom or Dad steps in and directs Edward and one of the younger children into a physical activity or a mind-challenging game that we keep a constant ear to, just in case intervention becomes necessary.

Probably the easiest thing we do to help minimize the "shut-out" feeling Rosa and Nathaniel get from Edward is to encourage them to "snuggle" with him while he's watching television. Although Edward will likely not respond any more than to occasionally put an arm around one of them, he doesn't object when Rosa climbs up on his lap or Nathaniel leans against him, and they feel accepted. It's not unusual to look in the living room in the hour or so before supper and see all three kids snuggled up on the couch watching Nickelodeon. And peace temporarily reigns.

With all the extra time and supervision Edward continues to require from Mom and Dad, the younger children sometimes feel slighted and less important. To try to alleviate some of these feelings, my husband and I have set aside a "story" time at the end of each day for Rosa and Nathaniel. They each have about 10 minutes of guaranteed uninterrupted time with each parent. We may read stories, talk, or maybe play a game. During this time, Edward stays in his room doing an activity of his choice. That way we can give the younger children our undivided attention, reassure them that we love them just as much as their brother, and let them know that they are just as important to us.

In addition to dealing with all of this, as parents of a child with Asperger Syndrome, we are also included in the negative attitude much of the world has about our son. We have been accused of bad parenting, being overly strict, too easy, overprotective, unreasonable, and demanding by educators, parents of our son's peers, and even family members. We often receive disapproving looks when in public because we cannot talk to Edward in the same manner we do our other children if we want him to hear us. While uninformed people's opinions in this area are a relatively minor concern to us, when paired with the fact that we can't leave Edward alone and we can't get sitters to stay with him, our social life is nearly nonexistent. Simply put, if we can't take Edward with us, at least one of us stays home.

Another part of daily life as Edward's parents is exhaustion. Having to be on constant alert and dealing with the thousand-and-one annoying things Edward does without realizing it takes its toll. Keeping up with a "typical" teenager can be taxing, but providing all the additional supervision Edward needs every day creates a large physical and emotional drain. Unfortunately, nighttime doesn't provide respite either, because Edward frequently can't get to sleep for several hours after he goes to bed, especially when his stress level is up. Knowing the unpredictability of his behavior, we can't sleep until he does. Even then we sleep lightly, always ready to react.

The largest single concern that always lurks in the back of our minds is our son's future. This concern grows daily as Edward approaches adulthood physically and intellectually, while still remaining a very young child in many of the basic skills necessary to be able to survive and succeed in the outside world. We look ahead and see that despite his intelligence, when our son graduates from high school in 2 years he will not be ready to deal with the demands of college or even a vocational school on his own. The same is true of employment. We don't want to see him forced to sit at home doing nothing because the world will not give him the acceptance, guidance, and accommodation he needs to be a productive member of society.

We also have to think ahead to the time when we are no longer able to provide what he needs. Unfortunately, at this time there is no place for people with Asperger Syndrome to go for assistance of any type because they fail to meet all criteria to be eligible. This is a frightening concern our family lives with, as we try to bring the plight and potential of individuals with Asperger Syndrome to the attention of the public.

Like all families we have good days and not-so-good days. True, our good days are more stress-filled than in an average family, and our bad days are like living in a war zone, but like most families the good days outnumber the bad. We have learned to cherish those infrequent moments when Edward gets all the pieces put together and responds appropriately or with thoughtfulness on his own—moments such as when we walk into a room to find Edward sitting on the couch with a rare expression of peaceful contentment on his face as his two young cousins with autism sleep curled up in his arms. We have also learned to appreciate and find amusement in some of his unique ways of looking at things. We look forward to those infrequent occasions when he realizes he did something well and feels proud of himself. We are impressed when something temporarily opens a window and he writes a poem with clear insight.

Most importantly, these rare moments remind us that under all the problems and aggravations, there is a good kid who wants very much to be like everyone else. And that gives us the hope and strength to go on for one more day.

 ## ANDREW

My name is Jo Ellen and I have a son with Asperger Syndrome. A year ago, I had never even heard of this syndrome, but now feel that I have tried to get my hand on every book, article, and piece of information that might help me understand my son and offer him the help that will guide him along in life. I am hoping that in writing down some of my thoughts and feelings, it might help other parents, families, friends, or teachers who are reaching out to the children who have Asperger Syndrome. Perhaps I can share some of the struggles and triumphs we have experienced with our son, Andrew, and perhaps in some small way help you through your journey.

Our son was diagnosed just a few months before his sixth birthday. My husband and I are educated professionals, he an engineer, and I a nurse. Andrew, the oldest child, lives with us and his 3-year-old sister in a middle-class suburban area. It has been only 7 months since we received the diagnosis, and a lot led up to it and a lot has happened since then. Actually, Andrew was one of the youngest children to be diagnosed with Asperger Syndrome, according to many professionals with whom we spoke. I worried that it meant he had a very severe case, but I think instead it was more our persistence and concerns that sought the diagnosis.

Andrew is a blonde, blue-eyed boy, who at 6½ is a whiz on the computer and loves to look at science and experiment books. He attends an all-day kindergarten program in the public school system, and although he doesn't much like the schoolwork part, he already reads on the third-grade level. He looks like any other kindergartner; it isn't until you are around him more that you begin to notice subtle differences in his personality. For instance, he does not have much eye contact with other kids, and he is very particular about not touching finger paints or anything messy. He rarely raises his hand in school, and often daydreams or gets a far-off look in his eyes. He has a hard time interacting with peers, and occasionally screams out when he is upset. Lately, he has taken to a sort of self-talk to himself during quiet times, sort of "reliving" conversations with others. He is working on his knock-knock jokes, and we read books together on social situations. He doesn't play much with other children. He has to wear only sweatpants (because they are soft), he much prefers foods that go "crunch," and he won't eat slimy foods. We always thought he was the ideal child—he would always entertain himself so well when he was just a toddler. Little did we know that this was something that might be a sign of things to come.

I thought I would share some things that I have found helpful, at least for me, in working with a child with Asperger Syndrome. I will give a brief history up to diagnosis and then share some things that we as a family have found to be helpful.

Andrew was born 5 weeks early after a somewhat complicated pregnancy with preterm contractions. He spent a week in the neonatal intensive care unit, because of a possible "seizure-like activity" that was proven negative with a CAT scan. He had no further neuro-logical problems and seemed to develop well. He was slightly behind at the 9-month checkup on some motor skills, but with the premature birth adjustment, he was on target. He was a late walker—14 months—but talked right on schedule. His only real illnesses were frequent ear infections, which were treated with ear tubes. He always preferred to play alone, look at books, and entertain himself. Our friends said we had the "perfect child." He never was much of a climber, never tried to get out of his crib, and was always a good eater. He did, however, do things like line objects up according to size and shape, and he recognized unusual things in his environment, like the tape dispenser could be a "6" or when turned upside down it became a "9." He began recognizing words at around age 3 to 4 years and could put them in their proper context.

We did not have any concerns until Andrew started 4-year-old preschool. His teacher noticed that he couldn't put on his own shoes. She told us that she was worried about his self-esteem if he couldn't dress himself, but it didn't seem to upset him. She also said that he just was not "normal" like the other kids, that he didn't play with them much, and that his behavior went beyond "unique." Every phone call she made to us was negative, and after awhile I felt that she couldn't see anything positive about our son. After several phone calls to us about our child's "unusual behavior," she suggested we have him tested through the school system. We did as she requested and they said he was "age appropriate."

As a mother I wanted to prove that Andrew was truly "normal," so I made an appoint-ment with a developmental pediatrician at the nearby university medical center. The doctor there found him to be healthy and within normal limits; however he was displaying some-thing she called "opposition behavior"; that is, he was defying us and wouldn't dress himself. She suggested that we see a psychologist to help us with disciplining him.

We made an appointment with a behavioral psychologist, who worked with us on time-out procedures. This seemed to help some; he too could see how bright our son was. Andrew still couldn't dress himself very well, and we had many a frustrating morning trying to get the shoes on. After four or five sessions with the psychologist, he suggested we have our son tested for autism at a "Multidisciplinary Team Screening." As a mother, I have to say that I was shocked. My son couldn't possibly have autism! Not my bright, wonderful son! What was this man suggesting, that my son had something major wrong with him?

The day of the testing I was more nervous than I thought possible. I told the speech therapist that I thought Andrew was tired, that he wouldn't perform well, that 3 hours in a row would tire him out, and that I wasn't comfortable with one test that would just label or diagnose him—just like that. She assured me that it would give us only information about how Andrew fit the autism spectrum, and would show where he did or did not have problem areas.

They gave us the results at the summation conference, just an hour or so after all the tests were completed. Andrew was not autistic. I breathed such a sigh of relief. He did, how-ever, have something called tactile defensiveness and dyspraxia (mild motor-planning prob-lems). I learned that he was nearly 2 years behind on gross-motor skills, and 2½ years on daily living skills. I went from relief to fear to guilt. After all those mornings of coaxing him to put on his shoes and timing him out for not dressing himself—I learned that he didn't have the motor-planning ability to do it. Boy, did I feel bad as a mother and sad too—making him try to dress himself. The poor little guy was not developmentally able to do it. I also learned that with his tactile defensiveness, he did not like messy things such as painting, touching gooey things, or even eating some slimy foods. We all came home exhausted.

The next step was trying to find appropriate help for him. I was disappointed in the testing site, as they were unable to provide me any therapy or treatment. They told me they were only a testing program, so I started calling occupational therapists listed in our phone book who worked with children. I found one who worked specifically with children, but due to insurance snags, we had to switch to another program. We were fortunate enough to have a children's hospital in the area and started with them. We have been very happy with the therapist there and have been visiting her for over a year now. She suggested that we retest Andrew for his gross-motor skills, so we had a physical therapist work with him. He was "age appropriate" after a summer of working on a few things like climbing the monkey bars, running, and jumping.

Andrew was now 5 and ready to start kindergarten; however, in light of his "problems," we decided to have him attend a prekindergarten class at a church-run preschool. The teacher was marvelous and made every effort to work with Andrew and us regarding our concerns. He was now in a class with eight other boys and a certified teacher. He still didn't seem to play with the other children and often screamed out when a bright light would shine in his eyes. He rarely participated in the lessons, although he was easily reading all the books the teacher had. At recess he preferred to spend the time up in the lookout fort lost in his own thoughts. The teacher clearly could tell that he was bright; she just didn't know how to teach him.

In October we had his first parent-teacher conference, and the teacher said she continued to have concerns regarding how he was interacting with the class. She said he seemed very happy, playing by himself on the playground or lost in his thoughts in the classroom. She already knew what we had done to date with his testing and therapy and was willing to help with anything that we suggested. I decided to call and see if he could be examined by another developmental pediatrician in town, but the wait was over 5 months. So in the interim we visited yet another behavioral psychologist, who worked with us on time-out again. They worked with Andrew and said he was pretty bright, and that we should try more positive praise. They also suggested that we invite other children over, one at a time, and have monitored play sessions. We were to praise Andrew for playing appropriately and time him out when he didn't interact well with the other child. This was challenging, as Andrew only lasted about 10 minutes, and that left Dad or me to interact with the other child for the remainder of the session. We even contemplated trying medication for Andrew's hyperactivity at this time, but decided to wait.

Our appointment with the developmental pediatrician finally arrived, and she was pleasant and very low-key. She took a thorough history from both my husband and myself, then worked with Andrew for a while. At the end of our session, she said she was not sure, in fact could not be sure until further testing by a clinical psychologist was completed, but she felt that Andrew had Asperger Syndrome.

It was something we had never heard of. I felt great relief, knowing that there was a physiological cause of some of Andrew's behaviors. Also, there was a deep sense of sadness—that I had lost my perfect little boy. I wanted to read everything. The doctor said that until the diagnosis was confirmed, she wanted me to read just one article. I remember taking it home, reading it from cover to cover, and saying, "Oh my god, that is Andrew." He didn't have some of the features some children with Asperger Syndrome have regarding memorizing dates, facts, or time schedules, but he always did like the United States map and could list most of the states. He definitely had trouble with eye contact and difficulty with social situations. These were his hallmark signs. He was hyperlexic and had some tactile defensiveness, which sometimes occur with Asperger Syndrome.

We were able to see the clinical psychologist within just a week, and she spent several hours with Andrew and me doing some paper-and-pencil tests and also some play therapy. She reviewed his history and asked me to return the next day with my husband, while leaving Andrew at home. The next morning we went to her office, and she confirmed that our son had Asperger Syndrome. Now the tears started to flow. I remember her telling us that we would need to "change our expectations of Andrew." But what did that mean? I then envisioned my beautiful son living at home with us well into his 50s, never getting a job, never marrying—all due to this syndrome and to his inability to understand social rules and participate well in our very social world.

The doctor allowed me to be sad, mad, and frustrated all at the same time. She was very supportive and suggested several articles, and she also left the door open for support sessions for us as needed. To date, I see her every 6 to 8 weeks for ideas on how to deal with Andrew's behavior, problems that arise at school, and ideas on how to cope with our special needs child.

For over a year Andrew has met at least three times a month with an occupational therapist, who works with his motor planning and tactile defensiveness. She has him paint with shaving cream (which he hates), and she has him make up obstacle courses and tell her how he would execute his way through them (which he loves). She works really well with him, and I am happy to report that just this month, she felt he was age appropriate for most of the skills, for example, using scissors, writing with a pencil. We continue to work at home with the tactile kinds of things, and he has improved steadily.

We had to make the choice of having Andrew start in the public school system or in the parochial school where he was preenrolled for kindergarten. After talking with both schools, we felt that he would be entitled to more services and have a better chance of having his special needs met if we chose the local public school. We met with the school district, which just a few weeks before school started wanted to have Andrew take all kinds of intelligence tests, aptitude tests, etc. He took them and did very well. The school district examiners were impressed with his excellent reading and comprehension skills but figured that his attention deficit might challenge the teachers. We were lucky that the school district had at least one other child with a diagnosis of Asperger Syndrome, so at least the administration understood some of what we were up against.

I met with the teachers Andrew would have. We selected the new all-day kindergarten program to lessen his need for transition and to provide continuity for him. We had to educate the staff about Asperger Syndrome, and they continue to work well with him and us as parents. The school had him tested with the occupational therapist on site, but as expected, he did not qualify for therapy. However, he did qualify for their speech therapist to come into the classroom and work with him on conversational skills with the other children. She even brings games and has him teach another child how to play.

Andrew also started private speech therapy sessions before the school year started. I found a therapist who works well with pragmatics and social skills of speech, and she has helped him on a weekly basis. He likes the games she plays with him and is working on practical things like ordering a soda at McDonald's.

Another thing that I have found to be very helpful is talking with other parents whose children have Asperger Syndrome. When we received the diagnosis, I asked our developmental pediatrician to connect me with another mother who had recently gone through this experience of diagnosis and treatment. She found a very positive woman in our community who just 6 months before we met had received the diagnosis of Asperger Syndrome for her 10-year-old son. Her ideas, sharing, and support have really been a boost. Also, our community just happened to start a support group for parents of children with Asperger Syndrome. We meet monthly, share ideas and frustrations, and laugh at what other parents might be horrified to hear. It has been a wonderful sense of strength to see that the little oddities of your child are not so unusual and that other parents are going through the same kinds of things that you experience.

One thing that I have learned is that you have to grieve the loss of the perfect child. As parents, we all have expectations for our children. I always assumed that our son would be an engineer or scientist. I hoped that he would marry a nice girl and have a family. I don't know if any of these will come to pass; I hope that they all do. Right now, there are days that I am just thankful that we have had a calm day. He gets upset easily if he spills milk on his shirt or makes a mess of any kind. He cannot tie his own shoes (thank goodness for Velcro). He still gets frustrated with zippers or buttoning his own shirt. He is working on buttering his own waffles and cutting his own meat. It continues to be a struggle to get him to do any kind of art or to write. Andrew still has a hard time sitting still at mealtimes (but then again, don't most kids?).

Andrew rarely gets invited to anyone's house, and when he goes I worry about how he will act or react. He doesn't share toys well and doesn't understand the social skills that most 6-year-olds live by. He doesn't understand teasing and so is the victim of several classmates' pranks. It breaks a mother's heart to see her child be the butt of jokes, but you deal with it. Andrew doesn't understand humor very well, so we watch "America's Funniest Home Videos" on television and talk about why things are funny. We also have selected several knock-knock joke books to give him something to share with other people (and his teachers are great to laugh at his jokes). He has a hard time in new environments, so we try to explain everything as we go along. He isn't able to transfer social rules from one setting to the other, for example, "No kicking at school" can't be translated for him to "We don't kick at the playground." We have to remind him in each new setting of how to behave.

Parents deal with getting the diagnosis for a special needs child in different ways. You both start to feel guilty and wonder things like "Did I give this to my child?" Both my husband and I tried to look back to our family trees, to see if somehow we passed it down from generation to generation. Fathers grieve and accept in different ways than mothers—it must be in how we are genetically built. I am not sure. I, as a mother, needed to grieve, to cry and talk it over with supportive family and friends. My husband, on the other hand, chose to be more self-reflective and to pursue the Internet for up-to-date information. Being in the health care field, I started reading all sorts of studies and technical articles. I wouldn't recommend them for most people, as they have a tendency to present the worst-case scenarios.

It is also hard to decide who you tell and how much they need to know. You would never want to hold back information from those caring for your child, but just how much you tell a neighbor or another child's parents is an individual call. Our families have been supportive and encouraging, and now that they know more of why Andrew gets upset easily or behaves the way he does, they are more accommodating and eager to help him excel in areas in which he can shine.

As I write this, Andrew is halfway through his kindergarten year. The school has 30-minute monthly meetings when we as parents meet with teachers and the behavior specialist to discuss concerns or ideas regarding our son. They say he is doing better socially and has even initiated interactions with some of his classmates. He still doesn't raise his hand to answer questions and doesn't appear to follow a lot of the schoolwork. However, his reading skills are fine, and he has even participated in art class a little more. They do not think that he needs medication for the attention-deficit disorder at this time, and that is just fine by me. They also have started to let him have 20 minutes a day of computer time as a sort of motivational reward.

We continue to see the speech therapist weekly, and I keep a log for her of things to spark a conversation with Andrew. We have good communication with the school, and I am already planning ahead for the first grade.

Suggestions I have for someone who has a child with Asperger Syndrome are to keep an open mind and read all you can, especially handouts from your psychologist or therapists. Find someone you can confide in, like a sibling or best friend. These people are invaluable, as are any caring listeners. Spend one-on-one time with your child doing an activity he or she likes and excels at. It gives the child lots of positive reinforcement for things he or she already does well. Look up current sources on the Internet, in the library, or at autism centers. Start a parent support group in your area. It is really great to meet with other parents, and you might be able to help them as much as they help you. Truly, do not try to predict your child's future, just live in the present. Each child with Asperger Syndrome is different, and each child is special and unique. The most important suggestions I could give for parents, family members, teachers, or anyone working with these truly special needs children are to be patient, love them a lot, and celebrate their little victories.

REFERENCES

American Psychiatric Association. (1994). *Diagnostic and statistical manual of mental disorders* (4th ed.). Washington, DC: Author.

Americans with Disabilities Act. (1990). Public Law 101–336.

Asperger, H. (1944). Die 'Autistischen Psychopathen' im Kindesalter. *Archiv fur Psychiatrie und Nervenkrankheiten, 117,* 76–136.

Autism Society of America, Inc. (1995). Definition of autism. *Advocate, 27*(6), 3.

Bernhardt, G. R., Cole, D. J., & Ryan, C. W. (1993). Improving career decision making with adults: Use of portfolios. *Journal of Employment Counseling, 30,* 67–73.

Bieber, J. (Producer). (1994). *Learning disabilities and social skills with Richard LaVoie: Last one picked . . . first one picked on.* Washington, DC: Public Broadcasting Service.

Brigance, A. H. (1980). *Brigance Diagnostic Inventory of Essential Skills.* North Billerica, MA: Curriculum Associates.

Brolin, D. E. (1992). *Life Centered Career Education (LCCE) Knowledge and Performance Batteries.* Reston, VA: The Council for Exceptional Children.

Brown, L., & Leigh, J. E. (1986). *Adaptive Behavior Inventory.* Austin, TX: PRO-ED.

Bruner, J. S. (1966). *Toward a theory of instruction.* Cambridge, MA: Harvard University Press.

Clark, G. M. (1995, September). *Transition planning assessment for students with learning disabilities.* Paper presented at the Pro-Ed Symposium on Transition for Students with Learning Disabilities, University of Kansas, Lawrence, KS.

Clark, G. M., Carlson, B., Fisher, S., Cook, I., & D'Alonzo, B. (1991). Career development for students with disabilities in elementary schools: A position statement of the Division on Career Development. *Career Development for Exceptional Individuals, 14*(2), 110–120.

Clark, G. M., & Patton, J. R. (1996). *Transition Planning Inventory.* Austin, TX: PRO-ED.

Dolch, E. W. (1955). *Methods in reading.* Champaign, IL: Garrard Press.

Donnelly, J. A. (1996, September). *Jobs we've lost and ones we've kept.* Panel of individuals with autism presented at the MAAPing the Future Conference, Chicago.

Donnelly, J. A., & Levy, S. M. (1995, July). *Strategies for assisting individuals with high-functioning autism and/or Aspergers.* Symposium conducted at The Autism Society of America National Conference, Greensboro, NC.

Downing, J. A. (1990). Contingency contracts: A step-by-step format. *Intervention in School and Clinic, 26*(2), 111–113.

Durrell, D. D., & Catterson, J. H. (1981). *Durrell Analysis of Reading Difficulty* (3rd ed.). San Antonio, TX: The Psychological Corporation.

Edgar, E. (1987). Secondary programs in special education: Are many of them justifiable? *Exceptional Children, 53,* 555–561.

Edgar, E. (1988). Transition from school to community. *Teaching Exceptional Children, 20*(2), 73–75.

Enderle, J., & Severson, S. (1991). *Enderle-Severson Transition Rating Scale*. Moorehead, MN: Practical Press.

Frith, U. (Ed.). (1991). *Autism and Asperger Syndrome*. Cambridge, UK: Cambridge University Press.

Fry, E. B. (1980). The new instant word list. *The Reading Teacher, 34*, 284–289.

Fullerton, A. (1993). *Development of a life decisions strategies curriculum to promote self-determination*. Unpublished manuscript, Portland State University, Portland, OR.

Gillberg, C. L. (1992). Autism and autistic-like conditions: Subclasses among disorders of empathy. *The Journal of Child Psychology and Psychiatry and Allied Disciplines, 33*, 813–842.

Gillberg, C. (1993). Autism and related behaviors. *Journal of Intellectual Disability Research, 37*, 343–372.

Gillberg, I. C., & Gillberg, C. L. (1989). Asperger Syndrome—some epidemiological considerations: A research note. *Journal of Child Psychology and Psychiatry and Allied Disciplines, 30*, 631–638.

Gilliam, J. E. (1994). *Work Adjustment Inventory: Measures of Job-Related Temperament*. Austin, TX: PRO-ED.

Gray, C. (1994, October). *Making sense out of the world: Social stories, comic strip conversations, and related instructional techniques*. Paper presented at the Midwest Educational Leadership Conference on Autism, Kansas City, MO.

Gray, C., & Gerard, J. D. (1993). Social stories: Improving responses of students with autism with accurate social information. *Focus on Autistic Behavior, 8*, 1–10.

Greenwood, C. R., Carta, J. J., & Atwater, J. (1991). Ecobehavioral analysis in the classroom: Review and implications. *Journal of Behavioral Education, 1*(1), 59–77.

Guerin, G. R. & Maier, A. S. (1983). *Informal assessment in education*. Palo Alto, CA: Mayfield.

Halpern, A. S. (1992). Transition: Old wine in new bottles. *Exceptional Children, 58*, 202–211.

Halpern, A. S. (1994). The transition of youth with disabilities to adult life: A position statement of the Division on Career Development and Transition, the Council for Exceptional Children. *Career Development for Exceptional Individuals, 17*(2), 115–124.

Hardman, M. L., Drew, C. J., & Egan, M. W. (1996). *Human exceptionality: Society, school, and family*. Needham Heights, MA: Allyn and Bacon.

Harris and Associates. (1994). *National Organization on Disability/Harris Survey of Americans with Disabilities*. New York: Author.

Hendrick-Keefe, C. (1995, Winter). Portfolios: Mirrors of learning. *Teaching Exceptional Children, 27*, 66–67.

Holland, J. L. (1994). *Self-Directed Search–Form R*. Itasca, IL: Riverside.

Holland, J. L., & Powell, A. B. (1994). *Self-Directed Search Career Explorer*. Itasca, IL: Riverside.

Hudson, F. G., Colson, S. E., & Braxdale, C. T. (1984). Instructional planning for dysfunctional learners: Levels of presentation. *Focus on Exceptional Children, 17*(3), 1–12.

Hudson, F. G., Colson, S. E., & Welch, D. L. H. (1989). *Hudson Education Skills Inventory (HESI)*. Austin, TX: PRO-ED.

Individuals with Disabilities Education Act. (1990). Public Law 101–476.

Johnson, B. A. (1996). *Language disorders in children: An introductory clinical perspective*. Boston: Delmar.

Kamps, D. M., Leonard, B. R., Dugan, E. P., Boland, B., & Greenwood, C. R. (1991). The use of ecobehavioral assessment to identify naturally occurring effective procedures in classrooms serving students with autism and other developmental disabilities. *Journal of Behavioral Education, 1*(4), 367–397.

Kanner, L. (1943). Autistic disturbances of affective content. *The Nervous Child, 2*, 217–250.

Kaplan, J. S., & Carter, J. (1995). *Beyond behavior modification: A cognitive-behavioral approach to behavior management in the school* (3rd ed.). Austin, TX: PRO-ED.

Keel, J. H., Mesibov, G. B., & Woods, A. V. (1997). TEACCH-supported employment program. *Journal of Autism and Developmental Disorders, 27*(1), 3–10.

Koegel, R. L., & Koegel, L. K. (1995). *Teaching children with autism.* Baltimore: Brookes.

Lord, C., & Venter, A. (1992). Outcome and follow-up studies of high-functioning autistic individuals. In E. Schopler & G. B. Mesibov (Eds.), *High-functioning individuals with autism* (pp. 187–199). New York: Plenum Press.

Manjiviona, J., & Prior, M. (1995). Comparison of Asperger Syndrome and high-functioning autistic children on a test of motor impairment. *Journal of Autism and Developmental Disorders, 25*(1), 23–39.

McCarney, S. B. (1989). *Transition Behavior Scale.* Columbia, MO: Hawthorne Educational Service.

Mercer, C. D. (1996). *Students with learning disabilities* (6th ed.). Columbus, OH: Prentice Hall.

Minshew, N. J., Goldstein, G., & Siegel, D. J. (1995). Speech and language in high-functioning autistic individuals. *Neuropsychology, 9*(2), 225–261.

Moran, M. R. (1982). Language development and language disorders. In E. L. Meyen (Ed.), *Exceptional children in today's schools: An alternative resource book* (pp. 91–118). Denver: Love.

Moran, M. R. (1995). *Teacher assessment for instructional planning.* Unpublished manuscript.

Myles, B. S., Constant, J. A., Simpson, R. L., & Carlson, J. K. (1989). Educational assessment of students with higher-functioning autistic disorder. *Focus on Autistic Behavior, 4*(1), 1–13.

Myles, B. S., Simpson, R. L., & Becker, J. (1995). An analysis of characteristics of students diagnosed with higher-functioning autistic disorder. *Exceptionality, 5*(1), 19–30.

Newland, T. E. (1973). Assumptions underlying psychological testing. *Journal of School Psychology, 11*, 316–322.

Newson, E., Dawson, M., & Everard, P. (1982). *The natural history of able autistic people: Their management and functioning in social context.* Nottingham, UK: Child Development Research Unit, The University of Nottingham.

Nolet, V. (1992). Classroom-based measurement and portfolio assessment. *Diagnostique, 18*(1), 5–26.

Parker, R. M. (1991). *Occupational Aptitude Survey and Interest Schedule.* Austin, TX: PRO-ED.

Parks, S. L. (1988). Psychometric instruments available for the assessment of autistic children. In E. Schopler & G. B. Mesibov (Eds.), *Diagnosis and assessment in autism* (pp. 123–138). New York: Plenum Press.

Piaget, J. (1959). *Judgment and reasoning in the child.* Paterson, NJ: Littlefield, Adams.

Quill, K. A. (1995). *Teaching children with autism: Strategies to enhance communication and socialization.* New York: Delmar.

Rehabilitation Act Amendments. (1992). Public Law 99-506.

Reisman, F. K. (1972). *A guide to the diagnostic teaching of arithmetic.* Columbus, OH: Charles E. Merrill.

Repetto, J. B., & Correa, V. I. (1996). Expanding views on transition. *Exceptional Children, 62*, 551–563.

Roberts, G. H. (1968). The failure strategies of third grade arithmetic pupils. *The Arithmetic Teacher, 15*, 442–446.

Rumsey, J. M. (1992). Neuropsychological studies of high-level autism. In E. Schopler & G. B. Mesibov (Eds.), *High-functioning individuals with autism* (pp. 41–64). New York: Plenum Press.

Rumsey, J. M., Rapoport, M. D., & Sceery, W. R. (1985). Autistic children as adults: Psychiatric, social and behavioral outcomes. *Journal of the American Academy of Child Psychiatry, 24*, 465–473.

Rutter, M., & Schopler, E. (1988). Autism and pervasive developmental disorders: Concepts and diagnostic issues. In E. Schopler & G. B. Mesibov (Eds.), *Diagnosis and assessment in autism* (pp. 15–30). New York: Plenum Press.

Sarkees-Wircenski, M., & Wircenski, J. L. (1994). Transition planning: Developing a career portfolio for students with disabilities. *Career Development for Exceptional Individuals, 17*(2), 203–214.

Schutt, P. W., & McCabe, V. M. (1994). Portfolio assessment for students with learning disabilities. *Learning Disabilities Quarterly, 5*(2), 81–85.

Silvaroli, N. J. (1986). *Classroom Reading Inventory.* Dubuque, IA: Wm. C. Brown.

Skrtic, T. M., Kvam, N. E., & Beals, V. L. (1983). Identifying and remediating the subtraction errors of learning disabled adolescents. *The Pointer, 27*(2), 323–338.

Smith, M. D., Belcher, R. G., & Juhrs, P. D. (1996). *A guide to successful employment for individuals with autism.* Baltimore: Brookes.

Sparrow, S., Balla, D., & Cicchetti, D. (1984). *Interview edition of the survey form manual: Vineland Adaptive Behavior Scales.* Circle Pines, MN: American Guidance Service.

Spivack, G., Platt, J. J., & Shure, M. (1976). *The problem-solving approach to adjustment.* San Francisco: Jossey-Bass.

Swaggart, B., Gagnon, E., Bock, S., Earles, T., Quinn, C., Myles, B. S., & Simpson, R. (1995). Using social stories to teach social and behavioral skills to children with autism. *Focus on Autistic Behavior, 10,* 1–16.

Swicegood, P. (1994). Portfolio-based assessment practices: The uses of portfolio assessment for students with behavioral disorders or learning disabilities. *Intervention in School and Clinic, 30*(1), 6–15.

Szatmari, P. (1991). Asperger's Syndrome: Diagnosis, treatment, and outcome. *Psychiatric Clinics of North America, 14*(1), 81–93.

Szatmari, P., Bartolucci, G., Bremmer, R. S., Bond, S., & Rich, S. (1989). A follow-up study of high-functioning autistic children. *Journal of Autism and Developmental Disorders, 19,* 213–226.

Szymanski, E. M. (1994). Transition: Life-span and life-space considerations for employment. *Exceptional Children, 60,* 402–410.

Tantam, D. (1991). Asperger syndrome in adulthood. In U. Frith (Ed.), *Autism and Asperger Syndrome* (pp. 147–183). London: Cambridge.

Thorndike, R. L., Hagen, E., & Sattler, J. (1985). *Stanford-Binet Intelligence Scale* (4th ed.). Chicago, IL: Riverside.

Vandercook, T., & York, J. (1989). The McGill action planning system (M.A.P.S.): A strategy for building vision. *Journal of the Association for the Severely Handicapped, 14,* 205–215.

Wagner, M. (1989, March). *The transition experiences of youth with disabilities: A report from the national longitudinal transition study.* Paper presented at the meeting of the Division of Research, Council for Exceptional Children, San Francisco.

Waterhouse, L., Morris, R., Allen, D., Dunn, M., & Fein, D. (1996). Diagnosis and classification in autism. *Journal of Autism and Developmental Disorders, 26*(1), 59–86.

Wechsler, D. (1991). *Wechsler Intelligence Scale for Children* (3rd ed.). San Antonio, TX: The Psychological Corporation.

Wehman, P. (1992). *Life beyond the classroom: Transition strategies for young people with disabilities.* Baltimore: Brookes.

Wehman, P., & Moon, M. S. (1988). *Vocational rehabilitation and supported employment.* Baltimore: Brookes.

Wesson, C. L., & King, R. P. (1992). The role of curriculum-based measurement in portfolio assessment. *Diagnostique, 18*(1), 27–37.

Wing, L. (1981). Asperger's Syndrome: A clinical account. *Psychological Medicine, 11,* 115–130.

Wing, L. (1991). The relationship between Asperger's Syndrome and Kanner's autism. In U. Frith (Ed.), *Autism and Asperger Syndrome* (pp. 37–92). London: Cambridge.

INDEX

Academic functioning, 17–35, 43–50
Adult-mediated social strategies, 83–84
Americans with Disabilities Act (ADA), 98, 99
Antecedent modification, 93
Aptitude/achievement tests, 14
Asperger, Hans, vii, 1
Asperger Syndrome
  characteristics of, 1, 2–7, 8–11, 28–29, 43–50
  conceptualization of, vii, 1
  diagnostic classification of, 2
  effect on families, 115–131
  etiology, 8
  prevalence, 7
  prognosis, 8, 98
Assessment, 13–41
  basic assumptions about, 38, 39
  ecobehavioral, 35
  formal, 104
  informal, 15–35
  norm-referenced, 13–15, 39
  report of results, 35–36, 37
  social and behavioral, 69–74
  training for, 38, 40
Assignment notebook, 62, 65
Attention-Deficit/Hyperactivity Disorder
    (ADHD), 44
Autism, 100, 101, 102
  spectrum of, 2, 11
Autism Society of America, 8
Autistic-like, vii, 1, 2, 8

Behavior contract, 87, 92–93
Behavior interventions, 86–96
Behavior problems, 5, 28, 46, 48, 50, 62, 63, 101,
    See also Power struggles
Behavior reduction, 93–95
Buddy program, 61, 62

Case examples
  characteristics, 8–11
  families, 116–132
Change, effect of, 48, 51, 52, 61, 65, 76–77, 97
Cognitive behavior modification (CBM), 87,
    88–90

Community-based instruction, 112
Curriculum-based assessment, 17, See also
    Assessment, informal

Diagnostic and Statistical Manual of Mental
    Disorders (DSM–IV), 1, 2, 7
Diagnostic teaching, 33–34
Differential reinforcement, 94
Direct instruction, 64, 82–83, 89
Discrimination training, 89
Distraction/inattention, 44–45, 64
Duration assessment, 70, 88
Dyspraxia, 128

Early release, 61–62
Employment, 99–100
Environment
  analysis of, 70–71
  structuring of, 74–78
Expectations and rules, 75–76

Frequency counts, 70, 88
Functional analysis, 71–74, 87, 105
Functional curriculum, 113

Generalization, 90
Graphic organizers, 56, 60

Hidden curriculum, See Instructional strategies
Home base, 63, 65
Homework, 65

Independent living, 101
Individualized Education Plan (IEP), 16, 102,
    103, 104, 107
  transition related, 104, 113
Individuals with Disabilities Education Act
    (IDEA), 98, 99, 102, 103
Instructional representation, levels of, 32–33
Instructional strategies, 51–68
  effective teacher characteristics, 67–68
  hidden curriculum, 66–67
  instructional sequence, 63–65, See also Scope-
    and-sequence approach

motivation, 65–66
structural strategies, 59, 61–63
teacher interaction, 67–68
visual strategies, 51–59
Intervention strategies
    assessment-based, 37–38, See also Behavior
        interventions; Environment, structuring
        of; Social interventions
Interval and time sampling, 70
IQ level, 43–44

Language, informal assessment of, 23, 25–26, 27
Learning disabilities, 6, 98, 99
Learning preference, 17, See also Student
    learning traits

Mathematics, informal assessment of, 21–23,
    24–25
Modeling, 64, 67, 81, 83, 89, 90
More Advanced Autistic People (MAAP), 121
Motivation, 16, 50, See also Instructional
    strategies
Motor skills, 7, 49–50, 66

Norm groups, 14, 39
Note taking, 56–59, 61

Obsessions, 7, 50, 66, See also Tunnel vision
Outlining, 56–59

Paid work experience, 104, 112–113
Peer-mediated social strategies, 85–86
Pervasive developmental disorder, 1, 2, 3, 9
Portfolio analysis, 34–35, 104
Postsecondary training/education, 101–102
Power struggle, 93, 95–96
Problem solving, 23, 48–49, 105
Processing difficulties, 28, 47–48, 82

Quality of life, 102, 105

Reading, informal assessment of, 18–21
Rehabilitation Act Amendments, 98, 99, 102
Reinforcers, 87, 88, 91
Response cost, 94

Rote memory, 46–47
Routines and schedules, 76–77

Scope-and-sequence approach, 17
Self-determination, 102
Self-management, 89–90
Self-stimulation, 7, 16–17
Situation Options Consequences Choices
        Strategies Simulation (SOCCSS), 78,
        79, 82
Skill acquisition, assessment of, 29, 32
Social autopsy, 82
Social/behavioral assessment, See Assessment
Social contracts, 87
Social interventions, 78–86
Social scripts, 79
Social stories, 78–79, 80–81
Splinter skill, 17, 21, 33, See also Scope-and-
        sequence approach
Stimulus overselectivity, 16, 28
Stress management, See Home base
Structure, 48, 74–78, 79
Student learning traits (SLT), 26–29, 30–31
Student strategies, 39
Student strengths and concerns, 36, 37
Support, 77–78

Tactile defensiveness, 130
Target behavior, 71–74, 89, 92
Timelines, 62–63
Time-out, 94
Token system, 91, 94
Transition to postschool
    assessment of, 103–111
    definition of, 97–98, 102–103
    life-span approach to, 111–113
    McGill Action Planning System (MAPS),
        105–107, 108–110
    need for planning, 98–102
    person-centered planning, 105–111
    planning process, 104
    portfolio assessment, 107, 111, See also
        Portfolio analysis
Tunnel vision, 45–46, 64

Visual schedules, 51–55, 61